Whatever Happened to Good and Evil?

Russ Shafer-Landau

New York   Oxford
OXFORD UNIVERSITY PRESS
2004

Oxford University Press

Oxford   New York

Auckland   Bangkok   Buenos Aires   Cape Town   Chennai
Dar es Salaam   Delhi   Hong Kong   Istanbul   Karachi   Kolkata
Kuala Lumpur   Madrid   Melbourne   Mexico City   Mumbai   Nairobi
São Paulo   Shanghai   Singapore   Taipei   Tokyo   Toronto

Published by Oxford University Press, Inc.
198 Madison Avenue, New York, New York, 10016
http://www.oup-usa.org

Oxford is a registered trademark of Oxford University Press

Library of Congress Cataloging-in-Publication Data
Shafer-Landau, Russ.
  Whatever happened to good and evil? / Russ Shafer-Landau.
    p. cm.
  ISBN 978-0-19-516873-0 (pbk. : alk. paper)
  1. Good and evil. 2. Ethics. I. Title.
BJ1401.S46 2003
170—dc21   2003048632

Printed in the United States of America on acid-free paper

For My Parents,

Bart and Barbara Landau

CONTENTS

PREFACE

We're right and they're wrong. It's as simple as that. . . .
Moral relativism does not have a place in this discussion and
debate.

—New York City Mayor Rudolph Giuliani,
Address to the United Nations General Assembly, October 1, 2001

I write these words only a few months after the September 11
tragedies. The consequences of that indelible day are still making
themselves felt, and will no doubt continue to do for as long as any
of us are alive to remember it. We can't anticipate all of the changes
resulting from the events of that terrible morning. But we can say,
with some assurance, that there has already been an important movement in the direction of our moral thinking. This shift has been little noticed, but is no less significant for that. It is a return to the language of good and evil.

Whatever happened to good and evil? Prior to September 11,
these notions didn't have the currency they once did. They struck
many as old-fashioned, as quaint vestiges of less skeptical times.
Many preferred to give up on these concepts; others were happy to
keep them, so long as the appropriate qualifications were entered.
We signaled our hesitations by declaring things right—for me; or
wrong—according to my culture. This sort of moral humility wasn't
entirely unappealing. But it was unsuited to issuing the kind of condemnations that we sought to express in the wake of the terrorists'
destruction. Those who perpetrated the attacks weren't just offending against our point of view. They were offending against the en-
lightened ethic of any person with a moral conscience. What they
did was evil.

Does that sound too strong? It may strike you as dogmatic, as
narrow-minded and parochial. If so, here's the natural follow-up:

Who am I to render such a judgment? After all, I'm just expressing how things appear to me. But why think that my perspective is any better than anyone else's? I see things my way; they see things their way. We're just different, that's all. And we have to respect differences. End of story.

In my view, that's a quite poor kind of story. It's one that's often told nowadays, one that has its persuasive advocates, but one that seems to me fundamentally corrupt. Admittedly, those who advance such a tale often do so from the best motives: intellectual modesty, tolerance, and an appreciation of cultural diversity. But these virtues fail to underwrite the views they are meant to do, as I will try to show in the pages to come.

The basic theme of this book is that some moral views are better than others, despite the sincerity of the individuals, cultures, and societies that endorse them. Some moral views are true, others false, and my thinking them so doesn't make them so. My society's endorsement of them doesn't prove their truth. Individuals, and whole societies, can be seriously mistaken when it comes to morality. The best explanation of this is that there are moral standards not of our own making. My aim is to show how that can be so.

ACKNOWLEDGMENTS

This book was written for those who might enjoy a little philosophical give and take, but who may not have much in the way of formal philosophical training. So it is appropriate, and no accident, that inspiration for writing such a book came from friends outside of philosophical circles. Foremost among these is Neil Salkind, challah maker and cookie baker extraordinaire, who just about dared me to write this book, and then, as I accepted his challenge, plied me with as much excellent chocolate as I could stomach. Though the book was terrific fun to write, his early encouragements made an enjoyable job even more so.

I was also encouraged by discussions with my dear friends Sheldon Whitten-Vile and Ron Schneider, both of whom took an interest in matters far distant from their professional concerns and indulged me in conversations about the topics of this book. I owe a different kind of thanks to an absolutely infuriating lunch with my good friend Andrea Katzman, who blithely rejected every single one of my claims, and in effect forced me to write this (attempted) refutation of her skepticism.

Much of this book was written while I was still at the University of Kansas, and I am especially grateful to Victor Bailey, director of the KU Hall Center for Humanities, for inviting me to offer a public lecture whose title gave this book its name. The enthusiasm that greeted that talk made me believe that there might be a larger audience for the ideas that are presented here.

A number of fine philosophers also contributed to making the book much better. Harry Brighouse and Brad Hooker gave me generous pats on the back, and kindly placed an earlier draft before the eyes of their students as a sort of test run. Peter Dalton, Greg Novack, and Paul Moser also read the whole of the manuscript, and provided me with many excellent suggestions for improvement. Walter Sinnott-Armstrong's often fatal criticisms had me revising well into the night—night after night. Of course it's painful to have one's work drawn and quartered, but there's no question the book is far better as a result of his scrutiny.

Having taught introductory ethics courses over much of the past fifteen years, I'm also now in a position to thank my many students, almost all of whom start off very skeptical of morality, and so bring to class the very kind of view that I am hoping to dismantle. In trying to place myself in their shoes, I am often reminded of my eighteen-year-old self, infatuated with Nietzsche and the French existentialists, absolutely convinced that the world as we knew it was inherently valueless. I'd like to think that it's the arguments to come, rather than my comfortable bourgeois existence and approaching middle age, that are responsible for easing me out of that sort of world view. I leave it for the reader to decide whether those arguments are in fact good enough to manage such a feat.

R.S.L.
Madison, Wisconsin

PART 1

The Status of Morality

CHAPTER 1

The Nature of the Problem

Here's a line I often hear: goodness, like beauty, is in the eye of the beholder. If I think something is good, it is. If you think it's bad, it is. Personal opinion is the measure of morality. To suppose that there are moral standards independent of such opinion—well, that's just wishful thinking, or an expression of arrogance. Clearly, morality is something that we made for ourselves. Others have come to different conclusions about how to live their lives. Who are we to say that they are mistaken?

Perhaps you feel the force of these thoughts. They've gained a lot of credence in the last half century. Despite their popularity, I think that they're fundamentally mistaken. I think, in other words, that some things are simply immoral, without qualification. Not because I say so. Not because my country says so. Not because *anyone* says so. They just are wrong, period.

That may sound like retrograde stuff. It certainly is an old-fashioned view. Yet most people, throughout most of human history, have found this a completely plausible position. Were they just unsophisticated? What do we know that they didn't, that could account for why so many people nowadays regard morality as a kind of make-believe?

There are a variety of factors that might do the explaining. Whether these factors also justify this skepticism is, of course, quite another thing.

There is first of all the loss of faith in traditional authority figures. Their edicts once served as moral bedrock for their followers. But we are nowadays far more willing to question the clergy, to doubt their spiritual integrity and to suspect their moral wisdom. And we've scrutinized our secular leaders within an inch of their lives. It hasn't done much to elevate their moral status.

There is also the greater exposure to other cultures, whose practices are incompatible with our own. It is harder to think of one's way of life as the only way, or the only natural way, when so many functioning, intelligent societies are organized along different principles.

Add to this the cautionary tale of our century's fanatics, whose certitude has cost tens of millions their lives. These people were convinced that theirs was the side of Good, that they had a monopoly on the Truth. Wouldn't a little self-doubt have been in order? If we have to choose between the hesitations of those who have their moral doubts, and the fanaticism of those who don't, then perhaps a bit of skepticism isn't such a bad idea after all.

There are also specifically philosophical sources of moral skepticism. If good and evil really exist, then why is there so much disagreement about them? Why isn't there a widely accepted account of how to make moral discoveries? Moreover, if there are correct standards of good and evil, doesn't that license dogmatism and intolerance? Yet if these are the price of good and evil, maybe we do better to abandon such notions. And doesn't the existence of good and evil require the existence of God? But what evidence is there that God exists? Doesn't the amount and degree of sorrow in the world, not to mention the scientific unverifiability of a divine being, give us excellent reason to doubt God's existence?

Taken together, these considerations have done a good deal to convince people to adopt a skeptical attitude toward moral claims. Without an answer to these (and other) worries, too many of us are likely to find ourselves acting and thinking inconsistently. Though firm in our conviction of a terrorist's depravity, we might, in other contexts, find ourselves claiming that our ethical views are merely our opinion, true (if at all) only relative to the culture we live in. The implication of this last thought is that those who disagree with us need not be making any error. When we think about concrete examples, of the sort that we were forced to contemplate on September 11, that kind of view can seem hollow and artificial. But the concerns that bring so many of us over the skeptic's side have yet to be dispelled. Until they are, we are likely to be morally schizophrenic: full of outrage at moments, and at other times just as full of reservations about the status of our moral condemnations.

My aim in this book is to display, and to undermine, the philosophical grounds for the widespread doubts about morality that have gripped so many of us. This aim shouldn't be confused with another one, also a central subject matter in ethics. I won't be selling you a story about what sorts of things are good and evil. I won't try to encourage you to praise benevolence and condemn torture. I assume you already do that, and don't need any convincing on that score. Rather than try to construct a list of moral principles that will distinguish good from evil, I want to ask whether any such list might possibly be *true*. You have your views about good and evil, and I mine. Are these the sorts of things that can be true in the first place? Could it be that both of our views are true, even though, at some places, they are incompatible with one another? Are they just true for me, or true for you? What could it mean to say such a thing?

In asking these questions, we are trying to decide on the *status* of ethical claims. We are not seeking to enumerate the things that are good and evil. Neither are we trying to spell out the content of moral principles: Actions are right provided that _____; motives are good just in case _____. Instead, we are examining the moral principles themselves. Are they capable of being true? If so, what makes them true? Where do they come from? Can we ever know which moral principles are true and which false? How is that possible (if it is)? What sort of authority does morality have over us?

No headlines here. The ethical matters that command attention typically involve efforts to decide what is actually right and wrong. The ethical issues that grab the public's fancy involve such things as the morality of euthanasia, abortion, capital punishment, etc. Yet everyone does have views about morality's status. People not only take a stand on whether, for instance, doctors may impart lethal injections to terminally ill patients, but also on whether such a stand can be true. And these latter views count. They are important in their own right. But they also have very significant implications.

Consider: those who believe that theirs is the side of Good, and that others are therefore Evil, may leverage such a view into one that allows the very worst sorts of horrors. We read about such people in our newspapers and history books, and see the fruits of their convictions in the body counts on the evening news. Such individuals justify their actions, to themselves and others, partly on the basis of their belief in a moral truth not of their own making. They seek moral authority in something greater than human choice, and take their confidence in having found it to terrible extremes.

It matters, too, that others are far more skeptical about the status of moral claims. If ethics is only a human construct, then what's to stand in the way of my constructing things so that only members of my family, sex, religion, or race get preferential treatment? If I'm free to invent a morality that suits my tastes, then watch out—some have a taste for blood, others for a social order in which they and their kind get to lord it over all the rest.

Of course, the view that good and evil exist only as human creations has also been prompted by just the opposite impulse, that of toleration. Here's the idea: if tolerance is as important as we think it is, then all ways of life are morally on a par with one another. And tolerance is, indeed, a very great value—if history has taught us anything, it is the need to stay the hand that would subordinate others just because of their differences. But why be tolerant of others if you've got it right and they're in the wrong? The value of tolerance is unimpeachable, but it also presupposes the fundamental equality of all moral views. If you value tolerance, you should reject the idea that there is a best or uniquely true morality.

Whether such a stand is correct or not, it clearly does describe an attitude of the first importance, one that is based very largely on a view about the status of our moral claims. As it happens, this defense of tolerance, as well as the moral crusader's willingness to crush his opponents, is a product of confused thinking. Those who embrace the possibility of an objectively true morality are wrong to suppose that this licenses the domination or killing of dissenters. And those who value tolerance are mistaken to seek its support in moral relativism and associated doctrines.

Part of my aim in these pages is to reveal the many popular misconceptions in this territory, and to display the real implications of our views about the status of morality. If I am right, then once we see such consequences clearly, we will be far less inclined to think of morality as a product of human invention. Certain things are right, and others wrong; some good, some evil; and we don't have the final say on what they are. There are moral standards not of our own making.

　　Whatever happened to good and evil? They never went away. We just thought they did.

CHAPTER 2

The Philosophical Terrain

Before we can appreciate the issues surrounding **moral skepticism**,[1] we need to make some distinctions, clarify some concepts. This is the part that philosophers love. Being the object of a philosopher's passion isn't all it's cracked up to be (just ask my wife), but in this case we have to defer to tradition and get clear on a few fundamental points. It won't be that painful.

One basic division within ethics is between those who do and those who don't advocate some form of moral skepticism. In general, a skeptical view is one that counsels doubt. Moral skeptics have their doubts about ethics. In particular, they deny that there can be an objective ethic—one that is true independently of what anyone thinks of it. For moral skeptics, morality is the product of human invention.

There are three basic kinds of moral skepticism. **Moral nihilism** denies that there are any moral truths. **Ethical subjectivism** claims that there are such truths, but that each person has the final say about what they are. **Ethical relativism** also allows for moral truth, but places its source within each culture, rather than in personal opinion; roughly, whatever society says, goes. Let's take these in order.

Moral nihilism amounts to the claim that there is no such thing as good and evil. Nothing is ever moral or immoral. The reason?

---

[1] Terms in **boldface** are defined in a glossary at the end of the book.

There are no moral truths; no true claims to the effect that something is right or wrong, good or evil.

There are two basic kinds of moral nihilism. The first is what philosophers call an **error theory**. Error theories imply that our moral commitments are always mistaken. According to error theorists, we are almost always trying to speak the truth when it comes to our moral pronouncements. But since there is no truth in ethics, we are invariably mistaken. Hence the error.

Morality could, on this line, simply be what religion was for Marx or Freud—a device to oppress the masses, to keep them in line, by fear of sanctions that don't really exist; or a set of superstitions and illusions, expressive of psychological infirmities, without any basis in reality. For them, talk of God's immutability, perfection, and omnipotence is all wrong, because it presupposes something (God) that simply does not exist. Likewise, for the error theorist, with ethics: we can speak of an action's virtues, but such talk, too, presupposes something (good and evil) that does not exist. It's all based on a fiction. And so our moral judgments are uniformly false.

Other moral nihilists are more charitable. These are the **noncognitivists**. Non-cognitivists deny that we are always mistaken in our moral talk. Not that they allow us the possibility of getting it right. Instead, non-cognitivists insist that moral judgments aren't capable in the first place of being either true or false. Such judgments aren't trying to describe things (moral facts) that, as it turns out, do not exist. So such judgments aren't always failing in their aim. Rather, moral judgments are designed to give vent to our emotions, to coordinate our responses with one another, to persuade others to share our feelings, to issue commands, or to express our commitments. And these ways of using language are not susceptible of truth and falsity.

When someone says that abortion is immoral, for instance, what she is really doing is counseling others not to have one. She is exhorting, persuading, encouraging. And these sorts of things can't be true or false. "Don't have an abortion"—that sort of claim isn't true. But it's not false, either. It just isn't the sort of thing that could be true or false, because it isn't even trying to report the facts. Non-cognitivists believe that moral judgments are meant to *prescribe*, not to *describe*.

What both kinds of nihilism have in common is their rejection of the existence of good and evil, right and wrong. This isn't to say that nihilists can't have preferences about things. They can: they might well prefer equality to racism, or enjoy seeing bullies get their come-uppance, or take pleasure in returning a lost wallet to its owner. The difference between nihilists and everyone else is not necessarily in their attachments, but in the attitude they must take to the objects of their affection. Whether we understand moral thinking in terms of invariably failed attempts to report on moral reality, or instead as disguised prescriptions or encouragements, the bottom line is the same. Nothing, really, is right or wrong, virtuous or vicious, good or evil. There are no true moral standards at all.

There are two forms of moral skepticism that are opposed to ni-hilism. Their opposition lies in the fact that both of these theories, subjectivism and relativism, accept the idea that there is some kind of moral reality. But they insist that it is a reality of our own mak-ing. Like nihilists, they believe that there can be no moral standards prior to human decisions about them. But unlike nihilists, they en-dorse the existence of genuine moral standards, since they believe that certain human decisions are sufficiently powerful to create a moral reality. And once we grant a moral reality, we also grant the possibility of moral truth. Moral claims will be true just in case they accurately depict the nature of this moral reality.

The first of these skeptical theories—subjectivism—claims that there is good and evil, but only in the eye of the beholder: what is good, is good for me, and not necessarily for you. Each of us is as trustworthy a moral judge as anyone else. We, each of us, get to cre-ate our own moral reality, and the truth of moral judgments answers to our own tastes and endorsements. According to subjectivism, my moral judgments are true just in case they are sincere, and so accu-rately report what I am feeling at the moment. So long as I really oppose terrorism, for instance, then my denunciation of it must be true. If I genuinely sing the praises of UNICEF, then the aid agency must be as good as I say it is.

The other sort of skepticism—relativism—also accepts the exis-tence of good and evil, but shifts the standard of truth from each in-dividual to society at large. According to relativism, individuals can make moral mistakes, but only because they have failed to note what society truly endorses. Social agreement is the ultimate measure of right and wrong. There is truth in ethics, and it isn't in the eye of the beholder, but rather at the center of social understandings. Creating genuine moral standards is a collective, not an individual, undertaking. Morality, in this way, is really no different from the standards that operate in the law or in etiquette.

Nihilists believe that there are no moral truths. Subjectivists believe that moral truth is created by each individual. Relativists believe that moral truth is a social construct. These three theories share the view that, in ethics, we make it all up. Prior to our decisions on moral issues, nothing is good or evil. Either morality is an elaborate fiction, and nothing is right or wrong, or moral truths depend exclusively on our (individual or collective) say-so.

These are the central skeptical theories that have earned the allegiance of so many of our contemporaries. But skeptics, as we know, aren't the only ones with views about the status of morality. Those who oppose them believe that there are correct moral standards (and thus that nihilism is false), and, further, that such standards are the product neither of individual preferences, nor of social agreements. (Exit subjectivism and relativism.) Those who think this way are known as **ethical objectivists**.[2]

Ethical objectivists believe, unsurprisingly, that ethics is objective: there are correct standards defining good and evil, and such standards are neither fictions nor human constructs. We don't, singly or together, have the final say about what is right and wrong. Ethical objectivists claim that even the ultimate moral commitments of individuals and societies can be mistaken.

For a claim to be objectively true, it must be true independently of what anyone, anywhere, happens to think of it. Mathematical truths are like this, as are truths in such areas as astronomy, micro-

---

[2] Not to be confused with adherents of Ayn Rand, who also call themselves objectivists. Rand's philosophy is one of admitted selfishness (she titled one of her books "The Virtue of Selfishness"—and meant it). Though she was also an ethical objectivist in common philosophical parlance—she thought that correct moral principles were not human creations—her specific version of it is only one of a hundred possibilities available to those who reject moral skepticism. The discussion of objectivism that follows is meant to be entirely independent of Rand's philosophy.

biology, and chemistry. We don't make them up. The true claims within these disciplines are not true because we think they are; we think they are because they really are. We may have invented the *vocabulary*, but we didn't invent the *fact* that (say) the earth is in a solar system, that genetic information is carried by DNA, that one oxygen and two hydrogen molecules will, at certain temperatures, bind to form a liquid.

I believe that moral truths enjoy the same status as the truths I've just mentioned: they are objectively true. It is still fashionable in many circles to dismiss such an idea as the expression of dogmatic attitudes, or as the product of outdated sensibilities. Yet as we shall see, objectivists are in the best possible position to resist dogmatism, and objectivism is, in fact, very well supported by much of what we currently believe. Indeed, the strengths of objectivism turn out to be extremely impressive.

Against these strengths (documented in Chapter 12), we can set the persistent worry: *just how* can moral truths be as objective as those of mathematics or the sciences? This is the ace up the skeptic's sleeve. Whenever we point to the many difficulties facing the skeptic, he or she can always reply by asking the objectivist, in effect, to put up or shut up. The skeptic has a simple, readily understandable story to tell about morality—we invent it all. Moral rules are products of our creative efforts, designed to reflect our tastes or interests. The objectivist view can't be this simple, and has struck many as too mysterious to be believed.

These mysteries can make skepticism seem the default position in ethics. Yet skepticism, though offering us a simpler picture of the ethical realm, is also vulnerable on many fronts. I believe that these liabilities are quite serious, and entitle us to shift the burden of proof onto the skeptic's shoulders. Once there, it won't easily be moved.

That's just talk, of course. Let's see what we can do to vindicate it.

PART 2

Against Moral Skepticism

CHAPTER 3

Moral Error

Throughout human history, individuals and societies have constructed moral standards to govern their behavior and to give expression to their points of view. We can call the fruits of these efforts **conventional morality**. Conventional morality is created by us and for us. Ethical objectivists do not deny the existence of conventional morality. What they insist on is the existence of a further, nonconventional morality (what philosophers call *objective morality*), which can serve as a standard for assessing the merits of conventional morality.

Many people, while voicing skepticism about objective morality, nevertheless embrace views that entail a commitment to its existence. One such view stems from the possibility of moral error. It seems to make good sense to suppose that conventional morality can sometimes be mistaken. Not every established practice is morally acceptable. No matter how deeply embedded in an individual's outlook or a society's constitutional essentials, accepted moral views might turn out to be wrong.

Isn't this true? Some societies are founded upon a principle that women are entitled only to those freedoms granted them by men. Others are founded on principles of chattel slavery that permit the ownership of fellow human beings. If conventional morality were all there were to ethics, then such practices would be perfectly aboveboard. We know these practices have flourished (and in some cases, continue to do so). They have been accepted as perfectly appropriate, even by many who have suffered from them. But that doesn't make them right.

There are two ways to account for mistakes in the fundamental elements of a moral code. The first way is that of the error theorists. According to them, *every* element of conventional morality is mistaken. So the basic moral views of the slaveholder and the misogynist are false. Good. But so are the those of the saint, the freedom fighter, the anonymous benefactor. Not so good. The radical moral equivalence embraced by error theorists is in fact one reason to be suspicious of their views. (More on this below.) When we claim, for instance, that those who demote women to second-class citizens are acting wrongly, we don't mean to imply that those who favor equality are acting equally badly. On the contrary. Our basic assumption is that moral mistakes can and should be *corrected*. Error theorists don't believe that is possible (except by abandoning all moral views).

The other diagnosis of fundamental moral error is given by ethical objectivists. If even the deepest moral convictions of individuals and societies can be mistaken, then, so long as there is any truth at all in ethics, there must be some standard, independent of such convictions, that exists to charge them with error. The importance of this point cannot be overstated. For this nonconventional, independent standard is just what objective morality is.

We can see this clearly if we contrast **internal** and **external critiques**. An internal critique is made from within a practice, an external one from without. Internal critiques do not challenge the fundamental assumptions of a practice. Instead, they take these for granted, and try to reveal any internal inconsistencies. Suppose that a society stands on principles of impartiality and equality. Then laws that violate this commitment are internally criticizable. Many citizens launched precisely this sort of objection to the segregationist laws that once mandated unequal treatment throughout the southern United States.

We don't need objective morality to level internal critiques. All these amount to, after all, is a claim that people are failing to conform to their own commitments. But don't we ever want to criticize the ultimate commitments themselves? For this we need an external critique—a criticism that does not content itself with pointing out internal inconsistencies, but rather takes direct aim at the fundamental assumptions guiding the practice under scrutiny. If these fundamental assumptions can ever be misguided—not just according to me, or my culture, but misguided, period—then (so long as there are any correct moral standards at all) there must be some objective morality that reveals the error.

If morality is thoroughly conventional, then moral standards possess the same status as traffic laws or the rules of card games. These can differ from region to region with perfect propriety. While we can always point out internal inconsistencies among competitors, we needn't indict those whose rules differ from our own. They needn't have made any mistake. Those who invent a variation on rummy, or require drivers to navigate the left side of the street, are making no error. There is a simple reason for this—there are no objective standards that could serve as the basis for measuring such error.

If we reject the possibility of objective morality, then we must say that our own basic commitments are *never* wrong (unless, of course, they are *always* wrong, as the error theorist maintains). We, or our society, are morally infallible, at least with regard to what we hold most dear. This must be so if our own ultimate commitments, or those of our society, are really the only moral standards there are. According to this way of thinking, the ultimate decrees of conventional morality cannot be mistaken. One might, of course, disagree with an element of a competing conventional morality, but that doesn't signal any error on its part. If conventional morality is the final word in ethics, then the wholly consistent Nazi, or the flawlessly rational terrorist, who perfectly embody their own conventional morality, are also perfectly morally virtuous, without moral flaw.

Error is still possible, even if morality is thoroughly conventional. Moral mistake would consist in endorsing or adhering to standards that conflict with your own (or your society's) ultimate commitments. But there could be no mistake in *those* standards—the ones that structure a society, or the ones closest to an individual's heart.

Thus subjectivism's or relativism's picture of ethics as a wholly conventional enterprise entails a kind of moral infallibility for individuals or societies. No matter the content of their ultimate commitments, these are never wrong. This sort of infallibility is hard to swallow in its own right. But it also generates a host of problems that significantly reduce the plausibility of skeptical theories.

CHAPTER 4

Moral Equivalence

Right off the bat, we can see that moral skepticism is a doctrine of moral equivalence. If there are no right answers to ethical questions (nihilism), or what right answers there are are given just by personal opinion (subjectivism), then any moral view is just as (im)plausible as any other. If relativists are right, then the basic views of all societies are morally on a par with one another. On all skeptical theories, the basic moral views of any person, or society, are no better than those of any other.

Moral equivalence has a democratic air about it. This can be refreshing, especially when contemplating the misery wrought by those who never doubt themselves. It's nice to cut such people down to size. But insisting on moral skepticism is not the way to do it. For moral equivalence is a double-edged sword. If skepticism is true, then no basic moral doctrines are better than any others. The blowhards and the self-righteous have no monopoly on the truth. But then neither do the saintly, kind, generous, and thoughtful. Their moral counsel is as good (or bad) as that of an ax-murderer or a child molester.

If moral truth is in the eye of the beholder, then those who see virtue in another's suffering or enslavement are making no mistake. Of course, neither are you, who oppose such things. But how comforting is that? *Regardless of what you take to be right and wrong,* don't you believe that those with just the opposite views are incorrect, are holding positions less plausible than your own? That must be false if skepticism is true.

Of course, just because others disagree with you doesn't mean that they are wrong. You could be the one making the mistake. Or you both could. The point is rather that while moral equivalence does sometimes sound attractive, it doesn't square with what we really believe. When we feel strongly enough to denounce something— terrorism, spousal abuse, torture—we don't for a moment accept the equivalence doctrine. We think our opponents are just wrong. And they couldn't be (nor could we ever be), if moral skepticism were correct. Their views, no matter how heinous or depraved, would be just as (im)plausible as our own. But who believes that slavers and abolitionists, for instance, are really holding views of equal merit? That slavery, or its abolition, are both equally morally acceptable?

Now, all moral criticism is launched from within some perspective or other. And some would say that, because such criticisms emerge from a specific perspective, then these criticisms are merely parochial, and cannot claim to capture the truth, or the whole truth. When we offer moral criticism, we do so *from within our own conventional morality*, which opposes in some way the one being criticized. And isn't ours just another outlook—not necessarily better or worse, just different? Who are we to say what's right and wrong? That we can offer an external criticism, one that takes aim at the fundamental assumptions of its target, doesn't prove that there is an objective, nonconventional morality. All it proves is that there are *many* conventional moralities.

Here is the truth in what was just said. Whenever you judge something right or wrong, you do so from your own perspective. Incompatible moral judgments reveal different perspectives. When we criticize those who go in for slavery, or those who would deny women an education or a vote, we do so from within our own, more egalitarian perspective. All true. But what follows? Not: therefore their perspective and our perspective are equally plausible. The Nazis have their perspective; we have ours. At this point it's quite open as to whether these perspectives are of equal worth, or whether one might be superior to another.

If all morality is conventional, then these perspectives are on equal footing. But from the fact that any moral claim is expressed from a particular viewpoint, it does not follow that all morality is conventional. That is just what has to be shown. We can't assume it from the outset, and we can't argue for it just by rehearsing the truism that all claims are situated within perspectives. After all, every mathematical and chemical and biological claim is situated within a perspective. When mathematicians and chemists and biologists disagree with one another, no one is inclined to say that they're all equally right, or that their claims are true just in case they (or their society) believe them to be.

As a general matter, though *every* claim is issued from within one perspective or other, it does *not* follow that each perspective is equally plausible. Nor does it follow that there is no truth awaiting our discovery. My views, issued from within my perspective, might be wrong, and yours, embedded within your own outlook, might be correct. Or vice versa. That's the standing, default assumption in all areas of inquiry. It might be wrong for ethics. But we would need a good argument to show it so.

One popular candidate for this task is the *Argument from Freedom of Conscience and Expression*.[1] It is given on behalf of those who favor moral skepticism and endorse the doctrine of moral equivalence. The argument begins with a widely accepted claim: we all possess equal moral rights to have and to express our moral beliefs. It proceeds through a crucial step: these equal rights establish the equal plausibility of our moral views. From these two steps alone it logically follows that everyone's moral beliefs are equally plausible. Equal rights entail equal plausibility; as a result, your opinion is no better than mine (or mine yours).

Despite its popularity, this argument does not work, and there is no way to salvage it. It starts off in the right direction, by recognizing equal rights to conscience and to freedom of expression. But then it makes an immediate wrong turn. The argument says that just because two people have an equal right to an opinion about a subject, their views on that subject are equally correct. But this principle is false. I have a right to an opinion about human physiology. So

---

[1] This argument and, subsequently, arguments followed by an asterisk, are summarized in the penultimate section of the book (see "Synopsis of the Major Arguments").

does my doctor. But these equal rights entail nothing about the plausibility of our views: mine are inferior. My right to think and talk about how an automobile is put together is just as valid as my mechanic's—but our views are certainly not equally plausible. I don't even know how to change the oil in my car.

The general point is this. Having a right to an opinion about something (physiology, auto care, the stock market, proper grammar, good and evil) is one thing. The plausibility of that view is quite another. Nothing follows about whether your view is correct, from the mere fact that you have a right to hold and express it. So even if it is true (as I believe it is) that everyone has an equal right to an opinion about morality, it doesn't follow that everyone's moral views are equally correct.

Moral equivalence sometimes sounds good in the abstract. But when we get down to cases, and contrast the views of Osama bin Laden with those of Mother Teresa, of Heinrich Himmler with those of the Dalai Lama, no one really buys such equivalence. This goes for cultures as well as people. No one thinks that the social code of Nazi Germany or Stalinist Russia was morally equivalent to that of contemporary Sweden or the Netherlands. These extreme examples make it clear that we reject moral equivalence, but we can stick with less dramatic ones to establish the same point.

No matter your stance on abortion or the death penalty, for instance, you don't seriously think that the views of those in opposing camps are just as correct as yours. They, of course, feel the same way. So, when push comes to shove, no one, really, puts much stock in the idea that all moral views are just as good as all others. Yet moral skepticism is committed to such equivalence. If nihilism is correct, then all moral views are on a par with one another (they're equally untrue). If subjectivism is correct, then everyone's basic moral views are as good as those of anyone else. If relativism is true, then the fundamental moral commitments of every society are no better (or worse) than those of any other society. When we examine how we actually go about the business of thinking morally, we find ourselves clearly opposed to such equivalence. Thus, if we are to be consistent, we should, with equal force, oppose the skepticism that generates it.

CHAPTER 5

Moral Progress and Moral Comparison

Moral progress occurs when people become morally better than they once were. Individuals are capable of such improvement. Penitentiaries originated as testament to this fact. Prisons were once designed to make convicts repentant, and so to register moral progress. If you visit Eastern Penitentiary in Pennsylvania, now a relic of a bygone penal philosophy, you can still see row upon row of solitary confinement chambers, the better to induce the desired moral reformation. It didn't always work. But sometimes it did.

Societies, too, are capable of moral progress. Most societies that used to tolerate slavery no longer do so. Many societies that once forbade girls an education now provide them one. We often treat the mentally ill and retarded much better than we used to. Certainly in all of these areas things remain imperfect. But compared to where we were a hundred years ago, we are leaps and bounds ahead.

It's not all good news, of course. We are also capable of moral regression—instances where we are no longer as morally admirable as before. Individuals can harden their hearts, indulge their pettiness, suffer moral corruption in countless ways. The moral constraints imposed by societies can crumble in any number of different circumstances. There is no invariant law of moral progress that governs the development of individuals and societies over time.

This all sounds commonplace, not even in need of mentioning, were it not for the fact that all forms of moral skepticism have great difficulties explaining the nature and possibility of moral progress and regression. This is further reason to be skeptical of skepticism.

With its abolition of moral reality, and hence of any moral distinctions, nihilism clearly removes any hope of moral progress. If there is no such thing as being good or evil—if "good" and "evil" don't denote a thing—then nothing can be morally better than anything else. It follows that nothing can be morally better or worse than it once was, since nothing was *ever* good or evil. Thus there can be no moral progress.

That said, nihilists can allow for three ways in which we can make some kind of progress relating to moral matters. First, we can abandon false moral beliefs (this means all of them, if error theorists are right). Second, we can erase inconsistencies among our beliefs; a more coherent set of views is, in some sense, better than a less coherent one. And, third, we can become better at achieving certain of our goals, including some that most of us take to be moral ones—that of reducing poverty, for instance, or promoting equality.

Crucially, however, nihilism does not allow any of these things to qualify as *moral* progress. Moral progress means being morally better than you once were. Being morally better implies some standard that measures moral improvement. But if nihilism is true, then there are no such standards. Hence, for nihilists, there is no such thing as moral progress.

Recall an earlier analogy with atheism. Suppose someone says that ever since you started going to church, you have come much closer to God. Now suppose that God doesn't exist. Then the claim about your new nearness to God cannot be true. That claim is meant to register some improvement. There is said to be some quality—nearness to God—that you now have more of than you once did. But if there is no God, then there can be no such quality, and so no possibility of improvement in that area.

Nihilists conceive of good and evil as atheists do God—there's no such thing. And so no such thing as being able to improve our abilities in these areas. Just as (if atheists are correct) we can never be nearer to God than we once were, we can never be morally better than we once were. Thus there is no such thing as moral progress.

It might seem that subjectivists and relativists could do better than this. After all, they do believe that there are correct moral principles. And these principles could serve as measures for marking moral progress. But they can't, really. The problem becomes apparent once we realize that such progress requires a *fixed* standard, that is, a standard that remains stable across the different contexts of comparison.

Suppose we say that you are now doing better than you once were. In what? Well, anything—in your running times, or your knowledge of foreign capitals, or your tendency to talk with your mouth full of food. What do we mean when we note your progress in these areas? Only this: that, relative to some stable standard, your earlier activity didn't measure quite as well as it now does. We are applying the same standard to prior and present conduct, and discovering that you now rank higher on the relevant scale (whatever it is) than you used to.

This is exactly how to measure moral progress. If there is such a thing, then there is some fixed standard that can be applied to assess earlier character and conduct, and to measure any improvement (or regression). Now in one sense, subjectivists and relativists can, in fact, allow for moral progress. But their vision of it conflicts with our deepest assumptions about what such progress amounts to.

The problem of measuring moral progress arises when we try to assess whether a personal or social code has improved over time. To make such an assessment, we compare the value of a code as it is, to its value at some earlier time. For instance, we compare the value of contemporary American civil rights law to the value of the segregationist laws that once prevailed. Or we compare the code endorsed by a newly penitent prisoner with the one that led him to his earlier life of crime.

Such judgments of moral progress (or regression) crucially involve an assessment of different, competing moral codes. There is the present code. And there is the former code. We have made improvement provided the present one is better than the old one. But making these sorts of comparisons is a very problematic proposition for moral skeptics.

There are two relevant possibilities when it comes to making comparisons of moral codes. The first is that we just can't do it. Nihilism goes this way, since all codes are equally untrue, but it might be an implication of subjectivism and relativism, too. Here's how that would work. Since (according to subjectivism) no one's moral views are any better than anyone else's, we can't compare one to another and say of either that it is better than its competition. Therefore we can't say that your present moral views are any better than the ones you used to have. Your former views and your present ones are in competition. If there is no way to arbitrate such matters, then there is no way to register moral progress.

One way to think about such a result is as a direct consequence of the moral equivalence that is allied with skepticism. If all moral doctrines are equal, then the one you presently have can't be any better than the one you used to have. And the one you used to have can't be any better than the one you have right now. Moral skepticism entails moral equivalence. Moral equivalence entails the impossibility of moral progress. Therefore moral skepticism entails the impossibility of moral progress.

We can say similar things about relativism, as applied to social codes—since they are all equivalent, none is better than another, and so all are on a par with one another. If relativism is correct, then the ultimate moral code of one society cannot be any better, morally speaking, than a similar code from another society. They are just different. Therefore a society's present moral code cannot be any better than the one it used to have. And the old one can't be any better than the new one.

Alternatively, we might preserve the possibility of interpersonal or intersocial moral comparison, and so of moral progress. But only at great cost. Any such comparison, including one of moral progress, must be undertaken by reference to some standard. If subjectivism or relativism is correct, then these standards must be either personal preference, or social agreement.

Now suppose it's December 31, and you are about to decide on a set of resolutions for the new year. Suppose too that your main goal is to become a morally wiser person. You mull things over, do an end of the year self-check. You want to pinpoint the room for improvement in your moral outlook. How do you do that? If subjectivism is correct, then you make the determination by reference to a certain moral standard—your own, existing, moral outlook. You

decide whether you've become wiser by applying the moral principles you presently subscribe to and seeing what they tell you about
yourself.

Societies, too, can go in for self-examination. If relativism is right,
then they can measure how far they've come in moral matters by
applying the correct standard for measuring such progress. And that
standard is none other than the one that currently prevails in that
society.

But of course this is terribly lopsided. It is a recipe for unfairness,
a classic case of stacking the deck. You determine progress by comparing where you are now with where you used to be. But any such
comparison requires an *independent* standard if it is to be fair. On
the skeptical accounts we are now considering, people and societies
are forced to assess their progress by importing their current moral
outlook and asking whether the outlook they used to have is as good
as the one they have now. This is a case in which a competition (here,
between past and present moral codes) is being judged by one of
the competitors. We don't allow that elsewhere, and we certainly
shouldn't allow it at the heart of morality.

Thus moral skepticism faces a dilemma. On the one hand, if all
moral views are equally (im)plausible, then none is superior to any
other. Therefore there is no way to register moral progress in such
views. On the other hand, we can register such progress, but only
by importing the conventional standards that are themselves the subject of appraisal. This leads inevitably to biased judgments of
progress.

So, on skeptical assumptions, assessments of moral progress will
be either impossible, or crippled by bias. Either way, moral skepticism cannot accommodate a plausible view of moral progress.

CHAPTER 6

Dogmatism

Here's a surprise: moral skepticism, not ethical objectivism, is the sort of view that allows the greatest room for dogmatism and intolerance.

A common criticism of ethical objectivism is that, if moral truths are not of our own making, then this gives objectivists license to criticize or belittle the moral views of everyone else. Those who are arrogant and overly self-assured about their moral views are almost always ethical objectivists. They believe in an objective morality, and believe, too, that they know exactly what it contains. (After all, if one thought that morality was just a human creation, why get so high and mighty about it?) The best way to counter this sort of smugness is to recognize that morality is all made up—either by each person, or by each society. Taking note of that should give one pause, and prevent the sort of moral arrogance that is so objectionable.

So goes the familiar story. But it goes wrong at two crucial places. First, there is nothing about ethical objectivism that mandates such arrogance. And, second, this kind of dogmatism is far easier to support if skepticism turns out to be true.

First point. Ethical objectivists believe that there is a set of nonconventional moral standards, standards that are true independently of what anyone thinks of them. From this alone, *nothing at all* follows about how to treat others who, in your view, have failed to light on the truth. We can see this by means of a simple comparison. We think that the truths of physics and mathematics are objective. But the objectivity of these areas does not mean that physicists and mathematicians are, or should be, arrogant about their views. On the contrary—the fact that they don't invent such truths should make them question whether their beliefs in these areas are really on target. The same point holds when it comes to ethics.

The correct posture of the scientist is that of wonder, occasional (or more than occasional) puzzlement, a recognition of the enormity of the task of understanding. Such respectful attitudes are possible only because one isn't inventing it all as one goes, but is rather trying to register the contours of an objective reality. In morality, too, the proper outlook to take toward an objective moral order is one of sometime puzzlement, an awareness of the complexity of the moral world, and a corresponding recognition of the limits of one's knowledge.

Contrast this with the various forms of skepticism that we have discussed. If nihilism is correct, then nothing is right or wrong. There are no moral truths, and so no truth to the effect that moral arrogance is wrong. Of course, you can still condemn the know-it-alls who make your life so miserable. You can say anything you want. But your criticism can't be true.

Still, nihilism will allow for a different, and fairly satisfying, criticism of the dogmatic person. Such a person assumes that his moral views are (obviously) true. And they can't be, if nihilism is right. All dogmatic people are making a mistake. Not a moral one. But a mistake nonetheless. They think they know what's right and wrong. They don't, because there isn't any such thing.

The problem for nihilists is that they are equal opportunity spoilers. The blowhards among us get deflated, and that's great. But so do the humble and inquisitive. Their views, like those of the pompous moralist, are likewise thought to be uniformly untrue. Whether a moral view is offered as God's only Truth, or in a tentative spirit of modest engagement, it can't be correct.

Subjectivism and relativism face a different sort of problem. These theories don't, by themselves, require people to be dogmatic. But both views make moral knowledge too easy to get, and so make it far likelier that people are right when they boast of their moral wisdom.

Think about subjectivism for a minute. According to that theory, a person's moral views are true so long as they accurately report what the person really thinks or feels. Since each individual is the measure of moral truth, there's little room for error. Admittedly, our sincere judgments can be mistaken, according to most subjectivists, if they conflict with other things we also hold dear. But apart from cases like these, we are never morally mistaken in our sincere moral evaluations. And so a very extensive moral self-confidence would be in order after all. The basis of modesty in other areas—the possibility that I might be far off base, mistaken in even my fundamental assumptions—is absent if subjectivism is correct.

Now consider ethical relativism. If this theory is true, then a society's ultimate commitments are what define right and wrong. This introduces more room for moral error, since people can be badly mistaken about what a society stands for. Still, anyone with a decent finger on society's pulse will only rarely make moral mistakes. The socially savvy have every reason to believe in their mastery of moral issues. And this leaves them little room for hesitation about their moral competence.

Certainly relativists could recommend, as a general matter, that we be cautious in our moral judgments. But two caveats. First, the reason for such caution could only be an uncertainty about whether we have captured what society really thinks. Our moral confidence should be proportionate to our knowledge of what society favors and condemns. So long as we've got it right on that score, then, according to relativism, there is no room for moral mistake. Second, the recommendations of any consistent relativist must always depend on what society endorses. If society's attitude toward moral matters is one of hubris and smug certainty, then *that*, and not an open-minded tolerance, is the morally required stance to take. That's a pretty shaky basis for resisting dogmatism.

Contrast these skeptical doctrines with ethical objectivism. If we don't make it all up, then there's greater room for error. If ethics is neither a comforting fiction nor a human construct, then answers to moral questions will be harder to discern. The harder it is to be sure that you've got the right answer, the less room there is for self-confidence—especially the extreme sort on display (say) in suicide bombers and Klansmen. Thus we do best to remain open to the possibility of correction. There are limits to such a thing, as there are limits to the tolerance that we can allow in any social setting. But there's no better check against hubris and arrogance than the recognition that we are not the authors of the moral law. Objectivists, not skeptics, are best poised to ward off criticisms that their theory sanctions dogmatism.

CHAPTER 7

Tolerance

Ask any ethics professor nowadays, and you are bound to get the same report—most students regard moral skepticism as the default position in ethics, and abandon their view, if at all, only very begrudgingly. (The exceptions are the committed theists, who make God, not humans, the author of morality.) Two reasons continually surface to explain their position. First, they are puzzled about just how morality *could* be objective. It's not as if they have knock-down-drag-out arguments for skepticism. Instead, they simply remain unclear about how objectivism could be vindicated, and believe—rightly, on the basis of such puzzlement—that some kind of skepticism is the only alternative.

The second reason is more concrete: students believe that they can sustain their commitment to tolerance if, and only if, they embrace skepticism. *The Arguments from Tolerance*° express their view succinctly. The first version goes as follows: If skepticism is true, then we must be tolerant of others. Skepticism is true. Therefore we must be tolerant of others. If my basic moral opinions are no better than yours, then I am not justified in intruding into your life and curtailing your liberties. According to skepticism, my basic moral opinions are no better than yours. And those of my society are no better than those of your society. Therefore we should keep our hands off. And a hands-off policy is nothing other than a recommendation of tolerance.

There are two problems with this argument. The first is that the argument begs the question. In assuming skepticism's truth, it presupposes what must be shown. This isn't an argument *for* skepticism—it's an argument *from* skepticism, and as such, is preaching to the skeptical choir. Thus it fails to supply a basis for objectivists to reconsider their views. The second problem is that even if the argument worked, it wouldn't show that skepticism *alone* could support tolerance. For all the argument says, objectivism, too, might be able to vindicate a policy of tolerance. We just have an argument purporting to show the compatibility of skepticism and tolerance. But that is not enough to undermine objectivism.

To defeat objectivism, we'd need a stronger argument. Here it is: those who value tolerance must embrace skepticism; we should all value tolerance; therefore we should all embrace skepticism. Where the first version says that skepticism *suffices* for tolerance, this one says that skepticism is *required* for tolerance. If you value tolerance, you must endorse skepticism.

Why? The account I often hear goes like this. Suppose that ethical objectivism were true. Then some personal and social ethical codes would be morally inferior to others. And so it would be OK to treat them as such. But that is intolerant. So ethical objectivism leads to intolerance. Thus if you value tolerance, you should reject objectivism. And that means embracing skepticism.

This account is mistaken. The supporting story says that if (as ethical objectivism claims) some moral views are inferior to others, then it is all right to treat them as such. But that doesn't follow.

Objectivists can distinguish two questions. First, are a person's (or a society's) moral views correct? And, second, if they aren't, then what should we do about it? The falsity of a moral view doesn't, by itself, imply anything about what response we should make. It doesn't, in particular, say that we should silence the view, take up arms against its proponents, enslave them, shun them, or anything else. The proper response to make to moral error is a very complicated matter, and can be settled only after more ethical investigation. Though some objectivists have used their platform to argue for very intolerant policies, objectivism per se is committed only to the idea that some moral views are right, and others wrong, independently of what we may think of them. It does not, all by itself, advocate any policy of suppression or intolerance. In fact, objectivists are able, as we shall shortly see, to argue that since tolerance is objectively valuable, we should all practice it under certain conditions.

Since that is so, it is doubtful whether tolerance requires skepticism. Indeed, there is excellent reason to suppose that tolerance is actually incompatible with skepticism. For if skepticism is correct, then either moral recommendations are never true (nihilism), or they are, but only relative to each person (subjectivism) or society (relativism). Now a policy of tolerance is really a recommendation. It tells us what we *ought* to do—be tolerant of others. But what is the status of such a recommendation? If we follow skeptics, then this policy, like all other ethical recommendations, must be regarded either as a fiction, or as a human construct. For those who value tolerance, this cannot be good news.

If nihilism is correct, then it *cannot* be true that we ought to tolerate those who differ from us. According to nihilism, nothing is really right or wrong. And so tolerance cannot be right. Intolerance cannot be wrong. We can have feelings about the matter, but these don't have any moral authority. And since there really aren't any true moral standards, no one's feelings—those of the racist, or those who welcome differences—are morally any better than anyone else's. Nihilism, as it turns out, is the weakest possible basis for a policy of toleration.

Subjectivism is only slightly better. It does require that we be tolerant—but only if we already value tolerance, or have commitments that imply a respect for others. Many don't. These many would rather silence opposition, censor the media, and burn books than live in an open society that tolerates diversity. If moral truth is in the eye of the beholder, then those who endorse *intolerance* are making no mistake. For them, intolerance is the order of the day. Burn those books (or heretics), expel or jail members of despised minorities. The intolerant are not just following orders. They are doing their duty.

The same sort of story will play itself out with relativism, only on a different scale. Relativism will require tolerance—but only for those societies whose fundamental principles require it. Societies built upon inequalities of various sorts, and others that are inherently repressive, are morally right to prosecute and persecute their targets. Those who advocate openness in such societies are doing wrong. For if relativism is correct, then moral truth is measured solely by conventional standards. Violation of such standards is the hallmark of immorality. So those who go against the grain are not to be applauded, but rooted out and shown the error of their ways. This is so no matter the content of conventional standards. Whether they call for tolerance, or, as is more frequent throughout human history, various kinds of intolerance, the basic social conventions must be obeyed. If you live in an intolerant society, then, morally speaking, you should be intolerant as well, and are wrong to push for anything else.

Those who embrace skepticism usually believe that tolerance is a good thing, even (and especially) for people and societies who denounce it. The need for tolerance is greatest precisely for those whose deepest impulse is to harm those who are different from themselves. Yet only ethical objectivism offers a secure basis for such a stand. Objectivists can say that tolerance is (within certain limits) a good thing, period. Its worth does not depend on whether I or my society happen to endorse it. That's too contingent a basis for defending a value as important as tolerance. If you believe that *everyone* is entitled to a basic kind of respect, to a certain amount of personal liberty, and to a core set of human rights, then you had better give up the idea that individuals or societies have the final word in ethics. Objectivism can reliably support these central moral protections. Skepticism can't.

CHAPTER 8

Arbitrariness

Few of us would feel secure with the thought that our deepest commitments lack any rational foundation. Yet skepticism ensures that morality is groundless in just this way. Skepticism sets morality on arbitrary foundations.

Standards are **arbitrary** if they are unsupported by sufficiently good reasons. Choices are arbitrary if there is no solid basis to distinguish one option from another. If skepticism is correct, then the moral demands we must obey are fundamentally arbitrary. That's because they are based only upon the arbitrary feelings of individuals or societies. Morality can have no legitimate authority over us if this is so.

Suppose there is a rock-bottom, fundamental law within society that you don't go around killing other people for sport. It's just not done. But what if you feel like a little hunting today? That nasty neighbor would make an easy target. . . .

Can such a thing be moral? Remember, we're not imagining a situation where it's either him or you, and one of you has to go. It's just that you wouldn't mind doing away with a damned nuisance. If nihilism is correct, then nothing is wrong, and so taking careful aim and following through wouldn't be wrong, either. The categories of right and wrong are simply make-believe concepts. We can use them perfectly well, ordinarily to coordinate our activities and often to try, perhaps surreptitiously, to influence others into doing what we want. But these concepts don't match up to anything real. *Right* and *wrong* aren't like *volcanic* or *right-angled* or *liquid*—concepts that describe real features of our world. Morality doesn't require you kill your neighbor, but it doesn't forbid you from doing so, either. If you're willing to accept the consequences, go ahead and shoot.

Subjectivism and relativism, by contrast, do insist that we are under various moral obligations. But these obligations are infected with arbitrariness as well. If subjectivism is true, then settling on what is right is like picking a favorite color. One's choice depends entirely upon one's tastes, and these tastes may be perfectly groundless. You like mauve? (Really?) That's disgusting, but only according to me, and my tastes are no better than yours. Morality is in all essential respects the same.

If we return to our hunting example, the reason (according to subjectivism) that you shouldn't squeeze that trigger is because you won't like the results. But what if you do? Then there's nothing wrong with preying upon your neighbor.

Suppose you have a high regard for personal trustworthiness, integrity, and loyalty. Then actions that realize these values are right. That sounds good. But what if you like betraying your friends or preying upon the weak? Then *those* actions are right. The basic problem, apart from the fact that subjectivism thus licenses all sorts of terrible behavior, is that the likes and dislikes that generate our moral obligations needn't have any rational basis at all. Those who enjoy seeing others hurt may have no basis for their attitude, but subjectivism does not require them to have any. All that's needed is that a person really, deeply approve of something. Whether the approvals are based on anything at all is (according to subjectivism) neither here nor there.

Consider this question: is it possible to value something that is unworthy of your affection? The subjectivist must return a negative answer. If value is in the eye of the beholder, then so long as you like something, it is valuable. It is valuable *because* you like it, rather than the other way around. To suppose that the object of your affections doesn't deserve such flattering treatment, you must first suppose that the object possesses a degree of value independently of your attitude toward it. But that is impossible if subjectivism is true. If all it takes to endow something with value is your approval of it, then such approval is morally all-powerful. It doesn't matter whether the approval is based on any reasons at all. That's why subjectivism is a doctrine of arbitrariness.

While this particular problem is solved if we move to relativism, a variation on the problem quickly arises. Relativists do offer a standard for assessing an individual's tastes; namely, whether such tastes accord with the prevailing cultural wisdom. But relativism has no standard for assessing the prevailing wisdom itself. A culture needn't have any reasons in support of its foundational creed. Or what reasons it has may, after scrutiny, seem appalling. Either way, no criticism can be made of the ultimate conventional standards. They are true by (relativist) definition. They cannot be mistaken, because their truth consists in their being endorsed. But a society's endorsements can be as ill-founded or as arbitrary as an individual's. Relativism does not alleviate the problem of arbitrariness.

Objectivism does. Objectivists eliminate the arbitrariness by claiming that both an individual's and a culture's basic allegiances are subject to rational scrutiny. In particular, objectivists claim that conventional standards can be true or false, as measured by a standard other than personal or cultural endorsement. Suppose someone hates homosexuals. Why? He just does—blindly, as an expression of a fundamental, unreasoning kind of disgust. This feeling, like all others, is subject to critical assessment. His disgust doesn't clinch the question, as subjectivism would claim.

Suppose a culture insists on the second-class status of women. This sort of inequality is one of the building blocks of many societies. The inequality is justified only if there are sufficiently good reasons for it. That most men, even most women, think it OK doesn't make it OK. They could be mistaken. Members of a subordinated group may come to identify with the interests of their oppressors. That doesn't prove the merits of the system; it proves, if anything, only the extent of the indoctrination that has allowed the oppressive regime to flourish.

In its insistence that even ultimate conventional standards are fallible, require good reasons for their support, and can rightly be demoted without such support, objectivism avoids the arbitrariness charge. A moral standard is nonarbitrary just in case it is supported by good reasons. The best possible reason to adopt a standard is its truth. And objectivism holds out such a possibility. Some of our commitments *will* be arbitrary, because they lack adequate support. But other of our commitments may represent success stories—they may be true, we may believe them because they are true, and so they will be well supported, rather than arbitrary. It is possible to escape moral arbitrariness only if ethical objectivism is true.

CHAPTER 9

Contradiction and Disagreement

A contradiction is a claim that is simultaneously affirmed and rejected, and so is said to be, at the very same time, both true and false. Any theory that generates a contradiction is false. This is a fact recognized in every discipline. If a theory yields a prediction that a heavy body will fall to the earth at a rate of seventy feet per second, and also that the same body, under identical circumstances, will not fall to the earth at that rate, then that theory needs adjustment (at the very least). As it stands, the theory cannot be true, precisely because it generates contradictory results.

If a mathematician claims that the square of the hypotenuse is and is not equal to the sum of the squares of a triangle's remaining sides, something has gone wrong. If a history book attributes the onset of the Civil War to Northern aggression, and then, on a later page, identifies the major cause as Southern aggression, then the author has bungled things. A contradiction reveals a fatal flaw in the underlying theory—no matter what that theory happens to be.

Logicians have shown, via a fairly easy proof,° exactly what is wrong with contradictions. The moral of their story: everything follows from a contradiction. In other words, to assert a contradiction is to commit oneself to the truth of all propositions, no matter how crazy or unrelated to the contradictory claims they happen to be. As long as I am willing to assert (say) that the earth is and is not a planet, then I am also committed to the claim that Winston Churchill was a woman, that two and two are thirty-nine, and that Cinderella was my maiden aunt. Best to avoid contradictions if we can.

As it turns out, both subjectivism and relativism generate contradiction. Subjectivism generates contradiction in the following way. Suppose you and I disagree about whether abortion is acceptable. So long as our true feelings are really being expressed, then neither of us is making a moral error. The one who says that abortion is acceptable is speaking the truth. It follows that abortion is acceptable. But the one who says that abortion is unacceptable also speaks the truth. It follows that abortion is unacceptable. So abortion is both acceptable and unacceptable. That is a contradiction.

Relativism generates a contradiction in the following way. Suppose one culture stands for the proposition that all people ought to be equals before the law. Suppose another culture insists that only all males are to be equal before the law; women ought to have fewer legal rights. Imagine that members of these different cultures engage one another in discussion. The views of each party to the debate accurately reflect those of his or her own society. Therefore they are true. But then it is at the same time true that men and women ought to be equal before the law, and ought not to be equal before the law. That is a contradiction.

Nihilism escapes this problem, because it refuses to allow for the possibility that moral judgments can be true. Since there is no moral reality to accurately depict in one's moral claims, there can be no moral truth. So moral judgments cannot be both true *and* false, because, according to nihilists, such judgments are never true. This ability to skirt the problem of contradiction is a definite plus for nihilists. But this advantage is purchased only by abandoning all hope that one's own moral convictions, or those of anyone else, are ever true.

If we left it here, the fact that both subjectivism and relativism generate contradictions would be a decisive refutation of their central claims. But we cannot leave it here, for these theories do have a way out. The problem is that the escape route carries with it severe difficulties of its own.

Here is the solution. Instead of the categorical, flat-out moral claims that we are used to, all moral judgments have attached to them a special (if implicit) qualification. When I say that something is immoral, I don't mean that it is immoral, period. What I mean is that it is wrong *for me*, or *according to me*. Or, if we focus on relativism rather than subjectivism, I mean that something is wrong *in my society*, or *according to my society*. The truth of a moral judgment is relative to the person or culture that issues it. We cannot know whether a moral claim is true without also knowing who is making it.

Note what this achieves. If people seem to disagree about some moral matter, then they needn't contradict each other. They can both be right. The contradiction disappears. Suppose I condemn suicide bombers. Others applaud them. Suppose also that I live in a culture that supports my view, and they live in a culture that supports theirs. The new tactic analyzes our judgments like so:

Me: As I see it, those bombers are wrong.
Or
Me: In my culture, those bombers are wrong.
Them: According to us, those bombers are right.
Or
Them: In our culture, those bombers are right.

We hear this kind of talk all the time. The hesitation, the qualification. Not wanting to sound dogmatic, we allow that things are right or wrong—but only according to me (or us). But what does such talk really mean? Only this: to say that something is wrong, according to me, is just to say that I think it wrong, or that I dislike it. It isn't really to say anything about the object of disapproval. In the preceding example, my condemnation of the suicide bombers doesn't describe them in any way at all. Rather than characterizing the bombers and their actions, the focus has shifted. I am instead just talking about myself (or my culture), issuing a report about my own sensibilities, or my culture's prevailing attitudes.

And what is the matter with that? It does solve the problem of contradiction. If all I do in making moral judgments is tell you facts about my own likes and dislikes, then you can perfectly well agree with what I say. In the brief Me/Them dialogue, I can agree with what they say, and they can agree with what I say. And isn't it so much better, all this agreement?

The problem with this is that the elimination of contradiction also signals the elimination of moral disagreement itself. If this strategy works, then moral disagreement is impossible. But moral disagreement is not impossible—it happens all the time. So this strategy fails.

Why does this strategy—changing the meaning of moral judgments, so that they always refer to my opinion, or that of my culture— do away with moral disagreement? Consider the potted example above. Will those who favor suicide bombings disagree with my claim? Why should they? They can readily accept that suicide bombing is wrong, according to Shafer-Landau. And I can easily accept their claim. If I think they are sincere, and not making some sort of sick joke, then I can accept as true that the bombers are right, *according to them*. But now there is no disagreement—I accept their claim, and they accept mine. There is nothing left to disagree about. So subjectivists and relativists have solved the problem of contradiction, but only at the cost of abolishing all moral disagreement!

In fact that is something of an overstatement. This strategy does allow for a small pocket of moral disagreement. But it can happen only if one party to a debate doubts the other party's sincerity, or their ability to capture what their society really endorses. For instance, in the Me/Them dialogue, the only way I could disagree with Them is if I thought that they didn't really approve of the suicide bombers. That is the *only* source of moral disagreement possible.

But this is pretty implausible. Think about the moral disagreements you have had. Didn't the disagreement persist, despite knowing that your opponents were sincere in their judgments? Indeed, if all they were saying is that they themselves felt a certain way, why would you bother to disagree? The very fact of the disagreement showed that, while you knew how they felt, you thought that they were mistaken (and vice versa). It is precisely this possibility that is excluded in the gambit to save subjectivism and relativism from contradiction.

Recall how we got to this point. Subjectivism and relativism generated contradictions. That falsified these theories. There was one way out—to alter the meaning of moral judgments so that they always, at least implicitly, appraised things according to the speaker (or her society). This eliminated the contradiction. Yet if things are now right or wrong, but only according to me (or us), then moral disagreement vanishes from existence.

Here again the nihilist has the upper hand among the skeptics. Not only can nihilists avoid contradiction, but the non-cognitivists among them are also able to account for most moral disagreements.

They will analyze such disagreement as emotional disagreement. Those on opposite sides of the abortion debate, for instance, *feel* differently about abortion. Some are repulsed, others are not. Some want to discourage women from having one, others have more permissive attitudes. If moral judgment consists solely in the expression of feelings, commitments, and emotions, then, since people differ in their feelings, etc., we can explain how people can morally disagree with one another without any threat of contradiction.

This is definitely a better approach than the one favored by subjectivists and relativists. But it will work only if genuine moral disagreement is always emotional disagreement. It often is. But it does seem possible for people to make sincere moral judgments without being emotionally supportive of them. Sometimes, for instance, people argue themselves into a moral position even if the view leaves them cold. Others see duty as a stern taskmaster that runs contrary to their deepest feelings. Still others are to some degree alienated from, critical, begrudging, or dismissive of what they take to be the correct moral outlook. These various possibilities make it dubious that moral disagreement is always emotional disagreement.

As we shall see (in Chapter 14), the widespread occurrence of moral disagreement is itself the basis of a powerful attack on ethical objectivism. Non-cognitivists can allow for the existence of such disagreement, even if their explanation of it sometimes fails. And non-cognitivists easily avoid landing in the lap of contradiction. Relativists and subjectivists, by contrast, either abolish moral disagreement, or retain it, but at the cost of contradiction. It isn't a happy choice.

CHAPTER 10

Relativism and Contradiction

Relativists are especially vulnerable to the charge that their theory generates contradiction. To see why, we need to ask a question that, to all appearances, seems trivial. Here it is: Can an act be performed in more than one society at a time, or is every action performed in just a single society?

The question certainly seems pointless. Or very easily answerable. It might appear that any given action—not a kind of action, but a specific, individual action—occurs at a particular time and place, and so occurs in just a single society. Relativists would love it if this were true. ⎣ *false*

Before we find out why, let me give an example to describe the kind of worry I'm thinking of. Suppose Luca Brasi receives orders from on high. Don Corleone assigns the hit, and Luca takes care of it. Where did the killing take place? In particular—which society did the killing occur in? Well, suppose it happened under the Brooklyn Bridge. Does that answer our question? Maybe. The bridge is located in the United States, so the killing occurred there. But it also occurred in New York. And in Brooklyn. OK, no problem yet. Even if we grant that these are each distinct societies, each of their social codes condemns Luca's act.

Yet it seems to make sense to speak of Luca's act as one that occurred within Mafia society, governed by the Mafia code of conduct. It isn't that great a stretch to speak of a Mafia culture, with its own ethos. The rules that comprise this ethos were regarded by many as *the law* that governed their lives. Obedience to this code, and so to the word of the Don, was simply understood, essential to a way of life that Luca, his family, his friends and relations all participated in.

Now the problem is acute. For if this description of what occurred is correct, then there is, after all, more than one society in which the killing took place. And these societies—Mafia society, on the one hand, and Brooklyn or U.S. society, on the other—issue different verdicts about the hit. If an action's moral status is determined, as relativists insist, exclusively by the conventions of the society in which it was performed, then relativism lands us in a contradiction. For Mafia society approves of the killing; the U.S. codes do not; and therefore the action is both right and wrong. That is a contradiction.

You might think this is just a trick. For the example I gave was an invented one, taken from a book and a great movie. But we can offer real-life examples that make the same point. Recently, a young woman was about to be forced to undergo a clitoridectomy. Her mother and her aunts were the ones doing the forcing. The young woman escaped, and brought suit against her family to ensure her bodily autonomy. She won.

This occurred in Paris, not ten years ago as I write this. The young woman and her family were members of an extensive community of Algerian emigrants. As is the rule with colonial wars, those who have sided with the defeated colonial power often emigrate to the mother country. This was what happened to many Algerians in the mid-1960s, when France abandoned its colonial aspirations in Northern Africa. In the major French cities there are now thriving Algerian communities, many of whose members still consider themselves bound to uphold and obey the traditions of their forebears.

Around the same time, a small group of members of a native American tribe in the state of Washington were convicted of violating Federal drug laws. They had used peyote in their religious ceremonies, something that their tribe had done for generations. The case went all the way to the U.S. Supreme Court, where their conviction was upheld. The Court held that a citizen's freedom of religion did not extend so far as to allow him to violate federal antidrug statutes.

Though the Court's reasoning invites scrutiny, the issue for us isn't whether their decision was the correct one. Nor do we need, for present purposes, to take a stand on whether forced clitoridectomies violate the moral rights of adolescents. The important point for right now is that these two examples seem to reveal a possibility that seemed only trivial or arcane just a moment ago. They seem to be genuine instances of an action performed in more than one society at a time. That girl was about to be strapped down in Paris. But she had always obeyed the laws of her emigré community, and certainly felt herself a part of that community. The peyote was used in Washington state. But it was also used in the context of a history of such practice, by a group of people who identified themselves with a cultural code that was centuries old.

There are subcultures located within any pluralistic society. And this creates a real problem for relativism, because we need to know, in such a case, which of these cultural codes is going to take precedence when it comes to making moral appraisals. The relativist tells us that an act is right if and only if it is permitted by the ultimate conventions of the society in which it is performed. But if it is performed in more than one society, it is governed by more than one code. When their elements conflict, there is contradiction.

So relativists have to do one of two things. They might deny that acts can be performed in more than one society at a time. But that flies in the face of examples such as the ones above. And it requires what no one has yet been able to do: to offer a definition of society that is so sharp in drawing social boundaries as to make it always impossible for an act to be performed in more than one society at a time.

The alternative is to allow that acts can be performed in more than a single society at a time, but to devise a rule for selecting which society's code should take precedence. But what will the rule be? Perhaps this: in cases of conflict, of the sort described above, always give the nod to the code of the larger society. So we judge Luca's killing a murder; we liberate the young woman from the threat of gross bodily violation; we lock up the peyote users. Regardless of whether you like these conclusions, there is a problem for the proposal. For why should we automatically favor the larger over the smaller group? Why should size make all the moral difference? The larger society is more powerful. It can enforce its decrees against the subculture. But might doesn't make right. Majorities sometimes make moral mistakes.

So maybe we should let the little guy win? In cases of conflict, allow the code of the subculture to take precedence in settling moral questions. But this, too, is unsatisfactory. For such a decision is as arbitrary as one that advocates majority rule. Don't we want the majority to intrude at times, especially when the minority culture is one that denies certain segments of its membership basic rights (to vote, to an education, to bodily autonomy, etc.)?

Here is a different solution. In cases of conflict, allow the protagonists to select which code they most identify with, and decide the moral status of the action by reference to their decision. But this is doubly problematic. First, in many cases, there is more than one protagonist. When Luca is about to kill his victim, do we consider Luca's wishes, or those of his would-be victim, in determining which society's rules should govern the case? Luca might identify himself first and foremost as a member of La Cosa Nostra. So it would be all right—required, even—to kill his victim. But his victim might see himself as most importantly a New Yorker, or a U.S. citizen. In that case, the killing would be governed by New York or U.S. law, which makes the action wrong. And so the contradiction would reappear.

But the real problem with such a solution is that it collapses relativism into subjectivism. If we let the individual choose which society will govern his actions, then we are making individual choices, not social choices, determinative of morality. That is subjectivism, not relativism.

The sort of problem cases we are focusing on are ones in which an individual, caught between two worlds, must choose between them. How is he or she to decide? The main obstacle to a satisfying answer is that *this choice is a moral choice*. Should the Mafia code or the U.S. code take precedence? Since this is a moral question, then, according to relativism, we must defer to society's rules. But which society? The one in which the act is performed. Which is that? Mafia society. And the United States. And each society will counsel that its own code take precedence over any others. Since that is so, we are right back where we started.

Those caught between cultures, situated in more than one, with plural allegiances, will rightly be puzzled about what to do when conflicts arise. Relativism cannot help them. It advises us to obey our society, but this isn't always possible. In cases of conflict, relativism gives us advice that amounts to contradiction. Any theory that generates contradictions is false. Relativism generates contradictions. Therefore relativism is false.

There *is* an escape path for relativists, though it is not without its difficulties. Relativists could just deny that there is such a thing as being right, without qualification. This isn't nihilism, because rightness, on this view, is replaced by the feature of *being right in the United States*, or *being right within the Mafia*, etc. Being right, on this account, is said to be just like being legal. On this view, there is no such thing as being legal, really. Rather, an act is legal within one society, and illegal within another. I am not contradicting myself by saying, correctly, that marijuana sales are illegal in the United States, but legal in Amsterdam. So, in Luca's case, for instance, what the relativist can say is that his carrying out the killing is right within Mafia society, and wrong within New York society. No contradiction there.

True enough. And, for relativists, this may really be the way to go, since anything is better than endorsing contradictions. But note the costs of such a move. First, it means that it would be literally impossible to ask a question that most of us think a very sensible one: is it right to obey the standards of my society? If there is no such thing as rightness, but only rightness relative to a society, then our question is either meaningless, or becomes a very different question. That very different question would be something like: is obedience to my society right *according to its own laws or customs?* The answer to that question is easy. The answer to our original question is often anything but. What this shows is that almost all of us do think that there really is such a thing as being right, full stop. When anyone caught between two cultures asks herself which one to side with, she is asking about what it would be right to do—not about what it would be right to do (say) according to Parisian society, or according to an emigré society (these have easy, obvious answers), but about what it is right to do, period. If that question makes sense—and it certainly seems to—then there is, after all, such a thing as rightness without qualification. And so this escape path would not work.

Further, insisting that there is only rightness within one society or other means that, again, there is great difficulty explaining the point and existence of moral disagreement. If all anyone could mean by judging something right was that it is right for one culture or another, then there would be no cross-cultural moral disagreement. In defending their use of peyote in religious ceremonies, the tribal members would be claiming only that such usage is right, within their own culture. In other words, that they endorse its use for themselves. But the federal drug agents obviously agree with *that*. And tribal members also, clearly, understand that such usage is wrong according to U.S. law. If all the federal agents meant when they denounced the peyote use was that it was frowned upon in the larger U.S. society, then there would be no basis for dissent on the part of the tribe's members. They knew *that*. But surely there is a disagreement here, and a point to continuing it and trying to resolve it. If there is no such thing as rightness, really, but only rightness within one society or another, then the disagreement disappears. Since it doesn't, we have excellent reason to think that there really is such a thing as rightness, full stop. And so we have a second reason to resist the relativist's escape route.

In short, relativists are faced with two unpalatable choices. If they allow, as I think they should, that there really is such a thing as rightness, then they are faced with contradictory assessments of some actions that are performed in more than one society at a time. They can avoid this fate, but only by rendering meaningful questions meaningless, and eliminating the point and existence of genuine moral disagreement.

CHAPTER 11

Is Moral Skepticism Self-Refuting?

Philosophers (and all other thinking persons) can't stand self-refuting theories. Such theories contradict themselves, and as we now know, any theory that issues contradictions is false. To be self-contradictory is to be in an especially awful position. For if a theory is self-refuting, then when we correctly apply the theory, it turns out that the theory itself must be false. By its own standards, the theory undercuts its own authority!

Here is an example. Suppose you seek my counsel in a matter of the heart, and I reply, confidingly, "You can trust me. Take my advice—all men are completely untrustworthy." If we correctly apply this view, it turns out that I, being a man, am completely untrustworthy. But then everything I say—including my claim that you can trust me—is itself completely untrustworthy. But if it is completely untrustworthy, then you can't trust me after all. If you can trust that what I say is trustworthy, then what I say is not trustworthy. Beginning to see the problem?

The question is whether moral skepticism suffers this terrible fate. And the answer is no. I know what you were expecting. But fairness requires an honest answer, and that is that moral skeptics need not contradict themselves.

But if that is so, why raise the issue? Because so many moral skeptics actually do end up with self-refuting positions. They don't have to. They can avoid it. But it's an easy trap to fall into, as is proven by the great numbers of those who have managed to do it. They make the ethical objectivist's job easier than it should be.

The path to perdition traces a pretty specific route. The basic pattern, which admits of variations, is simple, and can be formulated by the *Argument from Global Skepticism.*° The Argument is simplicity itself: **global skepticism** is true; global skepticism entails moral skepticism; therefore moral skepticism is true. Global skepticism is the view that there is no objective truth at all, anywhere. Moral skepticism is just the specifically ethical application of this wholesale doubt. If there is no objective truth, there cannot, obviously, be any objective moral truth. There is no objective truth. Therefore there is no objective moral truth. Moral skepticism is true because global skepticism is true.

Many people find such an argument appealing. Their attraction to global skepticism is usually conveyed in something like the following terms. Reality, it is said, differs from person to person (or culture to culture). What is true for me needn't be true for you. Before we came upon the scene, there was no truth. We don't just dictate what's good and evil; everything, every truth, is a product of human investment and creativity.

Why do people say such things? There are several reasons, but perhaps the most prominent one stems from the puzzlement people feel at trying to identify a uniquely correct perspective from which to view reality. This isn't a silly worry. But even if we fail to remove such puzzlement, this shouldn't lead us to take up moral skepticism.

Here's the idea. We all see things through our own lenses. So what strikes me as true, and what strikes you as true, may well differ, owing to differences in our perspectives. All of that is fine. But global skeptics go farther. If they allow that there are any truths at all, they will insist that truth depends on perspective. Since all judgments are assessed from within a perspective, so truth must also be relative to a perspective. Thus if your perspective differs from mine, your truths will differ from mine.

Consider the cosmological beliefs of the Kogi, a tribe located in remote Colombia. They assign the origins of the universe to a creator-goddess Mother, who, having impregnated herself with a wooden stick, imagined and then formed an egg-shaped universe of two symmetrical halves. Each half of the universe, itself shaped like a bee-hive, has four layers—in their center is our world. Each layer is in-habited by spirit beings; those of the uppermost layers largely benev-olent; those of the lower layers just the opposite.

We don't believe such a story, any more than we believe in the cosmological pieties that structured the lives of the Mayans or the ancient Greeks. Neither, of course, would members of those cul-tures put much stock in our story about the origins of the universe. The key point here is that the global skeptic will say that none of us has a lock on *the* truth, that is, a truth that exists independently of anyone's view of it. That's because there is no such thing.

Our cosmology works for us. It coheres with a broad set of be-liefs that we feel highly confident about. It is ratified by those we trust within our culture. Its constituent claims explain what goes on in the world in a way that makes good sense to those of us who be-lieve it. Of course, we can say exactly the same thing about the Kogi. The global skeptic concludes that what is true for us is not true for them. We each have our own truths. And to insist that there is some independent truth, some truth that obtains prior to any conceptual-ization of it, is just wishful thinking. It is also, often, an instance of insular thinking. Too often people suppose that theirs is the only correct way to see things, rather than appreciating the fact that what they see (and what they remain blind to) is a function of a parochial perspective that cannot have a monopoly on the truth.

Savvy philosophy students love to point out the problem in such thinking. From the fact that everyone sees things through different lenses, it does *not* follow that all truth is relative to these lenses. It does follow—really, it's just a different way of saying the same thing—that what people believe to be true will differ with their per-spective. Yet, as we will see, there might be objective truth about some issue even if people have intractably opposed beliefs about the matter. People might have absolutely irreconcilable differences about the origins of the universe, about whether there is some es-sential difference between male and female natures, or about whether abortion is immoral, and yet there can be, despite such dif-ferences, some objective truth that awaits our discovery.

That's just a promissory note (to be cashed in Chapter 14). Even if the defense there doesn't pan out, however, an absolutely fatal flaw remains for those who embrace moral skepticism because of their allegiance to its global cousin. The flaw is that global skepticism is self-refuting. We can see this clearly for each of the analogues of moral skepticism that we have been discussing.

Suppose someone is a moral nihilist, because he believes in **global nihilism**. There are no truths *at all*. That's why there are no moral truths. But if there are no truths, then what of the global nihilist's claim, that there are no truths at all? If there are no truths at all, then nihilism itself cannot be true. If we correctly apply the theory, it turns around and bites its own tail. If global nihilism is true, then there is at least one truth, and that is contrary to the claim that global nihilism makes. Being self-contradictory, it cannot be true.

Since global nihilism cannot be true, it cannot serve as a plausible basis for anything, much less moral nihilism. After all, if moral nihilism is true, then there is at least one truth (i.e., moral nihilism). And that contradicts global nihilism. So moral nihilists do best to look elsewhere for support.

A similar sort of story can be told for subjectivism and relativism. Suppose you are an ethical subjectivist because you have become convinced of **global subjectivism**—the idea that the truth in *every* area is in the eye of the beholder. If global subjectivism is true, then subjectivism about ethics must be true as well. But what is the status of global subjectivism?

Global subjectivism really amounts to the following view: A claim is true if, and only if, I believe it. Suppose global subjectivism is true. Now also suppose that I don't believe it (I don't). I believe that I am mistaken about some things, even though I don't, at present, know just what they are. I recognize my own fallibility, and so reject the idea that something is true just in case I happen to believe it. I think that global subjectivism is false.

According to global subjectivism, a claim is true if I believe it. Yet I believe this claim:

(F) Global subjectivism is false.

Therefore, if global subjectivism is true, then (F) is true, since I believe it. (F) says that global subjectivism is false. Therefore, if global subjectivism is true, then global subjectivism is false. Global subjectivism is not directly self-refuting, as global nihilism is. But once we add the true claim that someone (anyone) believes it to be false, then it contradicts itself, as we have just seen. Because it does, it cannot supply a plausible basis for ethical subjectivism.

Relativism suffers a similar fate. **Global relativism** claims that all truth is relative to a society. More specifically, it claims that a proposition is true just in case it is endorsed as such by a society, or is implied by a society's fundamental commitments. Global relativism is obviously the general form of which moral relativism is a specific instance. According to global relativism, there is no objective truth; no truth independent of social endorsement. Apart from the now-familiar worries about making social views infallible, and about the resulting inability to explain why societies would (or how they could) disagree with one another, we are faced with the specific problem of assessing the status of global relativism.

Global relativism is not directly self-refuting. But it must be false for any society that rejects it. And every society does. Consider a random sampling of predominant views held within U.S. society. The earth is round. Winter follows autumn. The Rockies are taller than the Appalachians. Does anyone believe that these true propositions are true just for us Americans? Or true only so long as we believe them?

By its own lights, global relativism must be false for all of those who are reading this and are situated in societies whose commitments imply a rejection of global relativism. If we correctly apply global relativism, then it can be true only if a society thinks it true. No society thinks it true. Therefore it is false.

The general lesson is that any effort to reject objective truth is bound to undercut its own authority. If a theory denies the existence of objective truth, then the theory itself cannot be objectively true. But then the theory itself should command the allegiance only of those who already believe it, or those whose societies already believe it. That is hardly a legitimate basis for endorsement.

If I reject all forms of global skepticism, but anyway ask *why* I should believe them, there can be no answer forthcoming. If global nihilism is correct, then there is no truth at all. And so nihilism itself cannot be true. If global subjectivism is correct, then it is so only if I believe it to be. If I don't, then it's false. And if it's false, why should

I change my mind and shelve my doubts about it? If global relativism is true, but my culture rejects it, then it is false. If we correctly apply the theory to itself (which is only fair), we find that the theory, if true, implies its own falsity, so long as a society rejects it. So, on the assumption that a society rejects global relativism (as all societies do), then such relativism, if true, is false. That is a contradiction.

None of this shows that *moral* nihilism, subjectivism, or relativism is false. What it does show is that a very popular argument for their truth must be scrapped. Those who arrive at moral skepticism via a global skepticism need to rethink their strategy. It just isn't plausible to say either that there is no truth at all, or that all truths are fixed entirely by the decisions of individuals or societies.

There must be some objective truth. If that is so, then why not suppose that some of it has to do with what is right and wrong, good and evil? That's the question we now need to turn to. So far we have confined ourselves to pointing out the failures of moral skepticism. But as everyone knows, it's far easier to criticize others than to adequately build up a positive view. We need to consider why so many have found moral skepticism so appealing. In particular, we need to defuse the criticisms of ethical objectivism that explain these allegiances. We can do this. Let's get to work.

PART 3

Moral Objectivity Defended

CHAPTER 12

How Ethical Objectivism Solves the Problems of Moral Skepticism

Ethical objectivism is the view that there are moral truths not of our own making, moral claims that are true independently of what anyone, anywhere, happens to think of them. In building a case for ethical objectivism, the first thing to do is to reveal how easily it solves the many problems that have plagued moral skepticism. Once this is done, we can then consider the outstanding criticisms of objectivism, and see whether they can be met. If I am right, we can turn every one of them, though some are certainly more difficult than others.

Ethical objectivism easily explains the nature of moral error and allows for everyone's moral fallibility. We can make moral mistakes, and often do, precisely because we are not the arbiters of what is right and wrong. Of course we each have our opinions, but these can be very wide of the mark. And that is because we are not the ones setting the mark. If we managed to create genuine moral standards, say, just by underwriting them in our practices, then it would be too easy to achieve moral perfection (including perfect moral knowledge). We are far from perfect, and ethical objectivism straightforwardly explains why that is so. We sometimes fail to adhere to correct moral standards. That is easy enough if we don't get to make them up.

Moral skepticism is a doctrine of moral equivalence. Everyone's views, whether those of Hitler or Mother Teresa, are morally on a par with one another. Ethical objectivism rejects this sort of equivalence. Objectivism per se does not tell us what is good and evil, whose moral views are on target, and whose off base. It tells us only that there is a set of right answers to moral questions, and that these answers, whatever they may be, are not of our own making. Since there are right answers, there are also wrong ones. If Mother Teresa's answers are closer to the truth, then Hitler's are farther from it. Objectivism will have no truck with the doctrine of moral equivalence.

Moral progress is measured by comparing two situations by reference to some fixed moral standard that can assess them both. We can truthfully say that we are better in race relations now than before just because we are comparing two periods against a fixed measure—in this case, a moral standard that dictates conditions of equality regardless of skin color or ancestral origins. Imagine that standard away, and do likewise for all other candidates, and there's no way to speak of moral progress. Condition the truth of that standard on my approval, or yours, or that of my society or yours, and so long as we are of different opinions, we again lose any basis for measuring moral progress. The kind of stable, independent standard required to determine moral progress is possible only if we assume that ethical objectivism is true.

Why not be dogmatic? It's a safe bet, so long as you're always right and never wrong. Moral subjectivism and relativism enhance the chances of being so. Ethical objectivism reduces them—drastically. Further, if you think that being dogmatic is a vice, or, if you don't go in for that sort of talk, at least unattractive and possibly even immoral, then ask yourself the following question: is it wrong just because I suppose it is, or because my culture thinks it is? Or isn't it rather that close-mindedness and a self-sure moral attitude are failings, even if I (or my society) came, perversely, to value such things? Only objectivism can allow for the possibility that dogmatism is bad even in those cultures, or for those people, who might find it attractive.

Is tolerance a good thing? Of course it is. Not unbridled tolerance—we shouldn't tolerate everything. Where should the limits of tolerance be set? That is an extremely difficult question. But not if moral skepticism is true. On skeptical assumptions, it's really quite easy—tolerance is of no value at all (nihilism); tolerance is good only so long as I think it is (subjectivism), or only so far as my society approves of it (relativism). These are the results of rejecting all moral authority, or placing final moral authority in the hands of individuals or cultures.

There's no practical problem if the person or culture in question is benign and broad-minded. But if you or your culture don't mind an occasional book burning or violent crackdown, then dissenters are well advised sit on their hands and keep quiet—anything else would be *immoral*. That is hardly the view of anyone who genuinely values tolerance.

Objectivists can, and skeptics cannot, declare tolerance a good for everyone, and every society. Though we must sometimes limit our indulgence of competing practices, we cannot, morally speaking, suppose that each individual, or each society, is always best placed to make that line-drawing call. People can make mistakes. It happened when they burned heretics at the stake. It happened three years ago when a woman was stoned to death for displaying her bare arm while driving in Afghanistan. If tolerance is genuinely valuable, and individuals and societies can err in their estimation of its value, then there must be some standard by which to measure that error—and that standard must be independent of persons and societies. Only ethical objectivism allows for such a thing.

Arbitrariness plagues moral skepticism. When appraising the bedrock claims that constitute the foundations of an ethical outlook, skepticism either denies that they can be true, or makes their truth dependent on individual or collective fiat, for which no reason need be given. An ethic may be centered around benevolence or justice, but it may as easily and as well be focused on preventing the distribution of pickled foodstuffs or ensuring that all cats get petted at least four times a day. This is the epitome of arbitrariness—*anything* that serves as an ultimate ethical principle is fit, by definition, to serve that role. Skepticism prevents us from making any rational assessment of ultimate ethical commitments.

Ethical objectivism, by contrast, allows people to avoid arbitrariness so long as their deepest commitments really are as valuable as they think they are. What's the matter with someone whose fondest hope and greatest care is to prevent the spread of pickles? Plenty. For our purposes, however, the answer is easy: there just isn't anything valuable in such activity.

Skeptics think that the worth of justice or the prevention of misery is no different, in principle, from the worth of constructing model airplanes or learning new napkin-folding techniques. The value of any such commitment is, for them, entirely a matter of our investment. If we are invested in toy models or making napkins look like swans, then bully for us. If we happen to care as much about global justice, then just as well. Neither commitment has any worth in itself, apart from our gracing it with our affections.

Now suppose someone is committed to justice and the prevention of human misery. Objectivists can rank these familiar moral virtues far ahead of—indeed, in a wholly separate class from—concerns with pickles, cat-petting, toy models, and napkins. That is because, from a moral point of view, principles espousing justice and the prevention of suffering are *true*. There are correct moral principles, and people who embrace them are not thinking or behaving in an arbitrary way. On the contrary. They are acting for the very best reasons there are. The commitments they endorse are correct, and not just because they or their culture happen to think so. Those who care about justice and human happiness are morally sensitive precisely because they are homing in on what really counts, rather than structuring their lives around pursuits with no intrinsic worth at all.

Ethical objectivism easily explains the nature of moral disagreement. Moral disagreement occurs precisely because people think that moral matters are *not* settled just by citing one's own (society's) feelings on the issue at hand. This is a perfectly general point about any disagreement. Physicists and mathematicians, for instance, wouldn't continue in their intramural debates if they thought that personal or social endorsement was the ultimate standard of truth in their investigations. Ethics is no different in this regard.

Ethical objectivism also easily manages to avoid the contradictions that beset subjectivism and relativism. If truth is in the eye of the beholder, whether a person or a society, then so long as people see things differently, there will be different, incompatible truths. That is the essence of contradiction. But if objectivism is correct, then, though people surely do see moral matters differently, they can't all be right. At least one party to any genuine disagreement must be mistaken. (It isn't always easy to determine who it is, but that's a different matter.) If they say that abortion is OK, and we say that it is immoral, or vice versa, then, since our endorsements don't automatically translate into the truth, we are not forced to say both that they are correct, and that we are correct. An independent, objective standard of truth saves us from contradiction.

Finally, ethical objectivism isn't even remotely threatened by chances of being self-refuting. Ethical objectivism naturally finds a home in a world view that says that much of reality is not of our own creation. One element of objective reality is an ethical domain, which includes truths about good and evil, and right and wrong. This picture is perfectly consistent with itself. It may not be true (though I obviously think it is). It might be, for instance, that there is an objective, physical world, but that there is no objective ethical one. Yet we can't criticize ethical objectivism for being self-refuting—it isn't.

Objectivists can and should take comfort from their invulnerability to the many criticisms that beset moral skepticism. Not only do they not succumb to these criticisms; they offer positive solutions to them that are attractive in their own right. Yet this is only half the battle won. The rest is more difficult.

It is always easier to offer criticisms than to reply to them and build up something positive. Now it's time to turn the tables and put the skeptics on the offensive. They have got a battery of concerns that, taken together, have convinced a lot of people that ethics can't possibly be objective. We need to face these worries squarely and see whether or not they can be met. I believe that they can.

CHAPTER 13

Universality, Objectivity, Absolutism

We can start the laundry list of skeptical objections with the one that is easiest to handle. The objection goes like this: if ethical objectivism is true, then two things follow. First, there must be certain **universal** moral laws that all people or cultures share. Second, whatever moral rules there are must be **absolute**. But there are no universal moral laws, and no absolute moral rules. Therefore ethical objectivism is false.

This is a perfectly logical way of arguing. Philosophers even have a fancy term for it—*modus tollens.*° Basically, modus tollens says that if some claim implies a second claim, and this second claim is false, then the first one must be false as well. This always works. Every argument of this form is logically impeccable. But, like all logical arguments, we can be assured of the truth of its conclusion only if we are first assured of the truth of its **premises**. And the premises employed in this skeptical argument are problematic.

To see this, we first need to provide just a bit of terminology. Universality first. There are two main senses of universality. The first says that a universal ethic is one that is *endorsed by* everyone, or every culture. The second says that a universal ethic is one that *applies to* everyone (even if they don't endorse it). Ethical objectivism denies that moral rules must be universal in the first sense, but agrees (with a qualification to be entered below) that they must be universal in the second.

Are there moral rules that everyone, or every society accepts? Maybe, maybe not. Though it's surely an interesting question, it is important to see that the fate of ethical objectivism in no way depends upon an answer. For objectivism is not a claim about which rules people *actually* accept. It's a claim, instead, about which moral rules they *ought to* accept. Objectivism says that people are obligated to act in certain ways regardless of whether they like it, or think that these ways are the best ways.

An ethic can be objective without being universally endorsed. Suppose that it is objectively true that the color of one's skin does not, by itself, make you a morally better person than someone with a different skin color. But this moral principle is not universal—it is not actually embraced by every person or every society. We can point to many instances where such a rule was honored, if at all, only in the breach. Surely if any moral principle is objective, the one I've just mentioned is a good candidate. Yet it is not universally accepted.

An ethic can be universally held without also being objective. Suppose that every society has some prohibition against killing, stealing, and promise-breaking. Even if that were true, it would not show that the authority behind such rules is objective. A relativist, for instance, would say that these rules are true, and genuinely apply to people, only because they are among a society's core values. On that account, the authority of these rules ultimately springs from the fact that they are endorsed by people. The values would be universal, but not objective. So ethical objectivism neither entails, nor is entailed by, a universally endorsed ethic.

On the second understanding of universality, an ethic is universal just in case it applies to everyone, even if it is not endorsed by everyone. It seems to me that an objective ethic must be universal, in this sense. An objective moral rule will apply to everyone who is able to understand and comply with its demands. (These rules don't apply, for instance, to cats, or to babies.) The actual failure of a person to appreciate the rule, or to comply with it, is not proof against its applicability. There is a genuine moral rule that prohibits chattel slavery, for instance. Many tens of thousands of slave owners failed to understand that there was such a rule, and failed to adhere to it. These failures didn't undermine the existence of the rule. If slave owning is objectively immoral, as I believe it is, then it is wrong for anyone to engage in it.

Now we confront a difficult challenge. For if moral rules are objective, and if objective rules are universally applicable, then all moral rules apply to everyone. But there seem to be many counterexamples to such a claim.

In certain parts of the world, it is unthinkable to make an offer of marriage without bestowing gifts of cattle upon prospective in-laws. Is this a genuine moral rule? I don't see why not. Yet the rule is not incumbent upon everyone, surely. I got engaged, and married, without giving any thought to offering such gifts. And (I'm pretty sure) my omission wasn't immoral. So this rule is neither universally endorsed nor universally applicable. Nor is it objective—if everyone stopped thinking of such gifts as mandatory, then the requirement to provide them would disappear. How can an objectivist say such a thing?

My view is that something can be a genuine moral rule only if it is objective and universal, or is *derived from* an objective, universal moral rule. There are countless different, permissible ways to fulfill the moral rules of honoring parents, children, prospective in-laws, spouses, the elderly, the dead, etc. Different societies will have different ways of specifying what fulfills such duties of honor. So long as these more parochial rules do not violate any moral rules, and themselves can be derived from fundamental moral rules, they seem genuine enough. But their bona fide status depends crucially on whether they are instances of moral rules which themselves are objective and universal. If they are not, then the objectivist must say that even if they are deeply and widely held, they are not authentic moral rules.

So not every moral rule must be universally applicable. In our society, it is immoral to toss sodden diapers at our dinner companions, cough into our neighbor's face, or take a scissors to the pants of strangers. But surely these strictures, though genuine enough, need not apply to every single imaginable person and society. And just as surely, the authority of these duties depends on the attitudes we take to them. (If we came to think of a cough in the face as a kind of warm greeting, then the moral rule forbidding such a thing would presumably disappear.) So these rules are neither universal nor objective. But if they are authentic moral rules, then they will be instances of more general moral rules that are, indeed, both of these things.

For instance, the rules I've just mentioned are very likely instances of a more general, objective, and universally applicable rule against causing unnecessary offense. What is offensive will depend partly on how people view the matter, and so will be partly a subjective affair. But the more general rule condemning offensive conduct must be an objective one, if there really is, for instance, to be a moral rule that prohibits diaper tossing and pants shredding.

So an objective ethic need not be actually endorsed be everyone, though it must apply to everyone. Some ethical rules are real, though neither objective nor universal. But this is compatible with ethical objectivism, because such rules are genuine only if they are instances of moral rules that are both.

And what of objectivism's relation to absolutism? Ethical absolutism is the view that there is at least one moral rule that is absolute, that is, never permissibly broken. Some people regard the prohibitions on killing innocents, or raping others, as absolute. Others disagree, envisioning rare, extreme circumstances where even such horrific acts as these might be morally justified, as the lesser of two evils. Thankfully, we don't have to try to settle that dispute here.

That's because ethical objectivism is a neutral party to that debate. Ethical objectivism is a claim about the *status* of moral rules. Ethical absolutism is a claim about the *stringency* of such rules. These are independent issues.

Does the moral rule prohibiting killing allow for suicide? For capital punishment? For shooting an enemy in a just war? These questions, all of them vital, do not touch the issue of whether moral rules are products of human invention. All the objectivist says is that the content of the moral rules is fixed independently of our opinions about the matter. Objectivism itself is silent on the question of whether moral rules may ever be broken. Our best ethical theory may tell us that certain exceptions to our moral rules are allowed. Yet the rules themselves, as well as the permissibility of breaking them on specific occasions, may, for all that, be authorized in some objective manner. So objectivism can be true even if absolutism is false.

And absolutism can be true even if objectivism is false. It may be, for instance, that a person or society insists on a blanket prohibition on lying. No lying is permitted, ever. Thus there is an absolute rule against it. But this rule might derive its authority just from personal endorsement (subjectivism) or social agreement (relativism). So ethical absolutism might be true even if ethical objectivism were not.

Thus ethical objectivism is not, after all, committed to unbreakable, absolute moral rules. It allows for their existence (if there are any), but is also compatible with views that permit us to break moral rules if the circumstances are dire enough. Objectivism is not committed to there being any moral rules that are universally endorsed. It *is* committed to the existence of moral rules that apply to everyone, though it can also, sensibly, allow for some that aren't.

CHAPTER 14

The (Un)Importance of Moral Disagreement

Will the debates about the morality of abortion, euthanasia, or capital punishment *ever* be resolved? Probably not. People have been disagreeing with each other about ethical matters ever since there were people around to disagree with. It's possible that things will change in the future. But not very likely. What lesson should we draw from this prognosis?

The *Argument from Disagreement*° tells us that if two open-minded, intelligent individuals persistently disagree about some issue, then there's no objective truth about that issue—it's just a matter of opinion. In ethics, of course, there are countless instances of disagreement, even among those who are fair, open-minded, and well informed about the relevant issues. If the Argument is sound, then from these assumptions it follows that there is no objective truth in morality. Perhaps there isn't any moral truth at all. Or what truth there is is fixed by personal or cultural opinion.

Despite its popularity, this classic skeptical argument is fatally flawed. Both of its central premises are shaky. First off, the extent of moral disagreement is often exaggerated. The really contentious ethical issues are the ones getting all the publicity, but this only masks the breadth of agreement there is on moral matters. Indeed, we couldn't go on as social animals were we not largely agreed on ethical fundamentals. Most of ethics is common ground. It's only a relatively few ethical issues that serve as the focus of intractable disagreement.

Still, that there are such disagreements cannot be doubted, and if it were true that their existence signaled a lack of objective truth, then moral skepticism (at least with regard to those disputed issues) would be vindicated. But it isn't true. Open-minded, well-informed physicists disagree about the basic building blocks of matter. This doesn't mean that there is no objective truth about that topic—that either there is no truth in physics, or what truth there is depends solely on one's perspective. There is a true model of the universe's physical constituents. I don't know what it is. Maybe no one does. The best theories we have may be way off base. But we aren't entitled to conclude, from the fact that even brilliant physicists disagree amongst themselves, that there are no objective truths within fundamental physics.

Skeptics might concede as much. They can amend the Argument from Disagreement and allow that intractable disagreement among intelligent parties does not *entail* skepticism. Still, they might argue, such disagreement does provide excellent evidence for skepticism, especially if the range of disagreement is very wide and the nature of the disagreement very deep. And now the ethical objectivist is in trouble. For, compared to the disagreements within the natural sciences, those in ethics are especially widespread and do go especially deep.

So: disagreement per se isn't enough to warrant skepticism. There is a correct physical theory, despite disagreements among physicists. But ethics is relevantly different. The amount of disagreement within ethics is far greater than that within any of the natural sciences. And you know what explains this? (You do.) The fact that ethics is all made up, and physics, or chemistry, or geology, isn't. There are objective truths about waves and particles, about molecular constitution, about the age of rock strata. The widespread agreement in the natural sciences is best explained by their converging on a set of objective truths.

Ethics, by contrast, is far more riven with disagreements. For instance, when we asked, just a moment ago, whether disagreement on hot-button issues such as abortion and euthanasia was ever likely to be resolved, the answer was: probably not. Yet if we ask whether there is ultimately going to be agreement about today's scientific puzzles, the answer is just the opposite—with time and energy, there is very probably going to be consensus achieved within the scientific community. This difference calls for explanation.

A skeptical diagnosis gains strength from this comparison, and can therefore be weakened to the extent that we can explain moral disagreement as some sort of remediable failure on our part. The idea is that if we were just able to improve ourselves in various ways, then we might manage to narrow the scope of moral disagreement to the level we find in scientific circles. If that were so, then the basis for the damaging disanalogy with science would be gone, and ethics might achieve a status equal to that of science.

Such a scenario isn't that far from the mark. Much ethical disagreement can be explained by people's lacking adequate information, or failing to logically think through the information they have. There would be far less disagreement about (say) the merits of welfare policy, or the legalization of marijuana, if all parties to the debates had their facts in order, and thought them through in a consistent fashion.

Yet moral disagreements will persist even if people manage to achieve this high level of thoughtfulness. And the scope of such disagreement will probably exceed that found in the natural sciences. Another factor that helps to explain this is that most of us are far less imaginative than we might be. In particular, we often fail to imaginatively place ourselves in relevant situations—usually, but not always, the situation of those who stand to suffer at our hands. Were we better on this score, this would cause the scope of moral disagreement to shrink even further.

One last factor: there is usually much more at stake in ethical matters than in scientific ones. This has the effect of importing bias and undermining neutrality, in a way that can help to explain the greater degree of disagreement within ethics. When scientific issues become intertwined with matters of prestige, the distribution of resources, and the allocation of respect, we see a commensurate rise in the level of disagreement about them. Once we correct for this sort of bias, we might be able to dramatically reduce the amount of disagreement, whether in science or in ethics.

Consider: who first identified the AIDS virus? You'd think that was a straightforward, objective question. But the amount of research money, fame, and (potentially) a Nobel prize at stake made this an intractable question within the biomedical community. What sort of intelligence does an IQ test measure, and what are we to make of correlations between test results and sex, race, or ethnicity? Again, apparently a straightforward scientific question. But as everyone knows, this has been a terribly contentious area that has generated little agreement. Is the best explanation of this that there is no objective truth of the matter? Or isn't it rather that so much hangs in the balance, and that the very high stakes involved tend to encourage partisanship and a lack of impartiality? It is no wonder, then, that the ethical issues of major importance have attracted a similar amount of conflict. Since we don't suppose that such disagreements within the scientific community indicate a lack of objective truth, perhaps we ought to be less confident about drawing skeptical conclusions when we encounter disagreements in ethics.

Greater information, better processing of that information, improved imaginative capacities, and an appreciation of the biasing influence that high stakes can bring would all, taken together, greatly diminish the degree of moral disagreement. Would the resulting disagreement still exceed the scope of that found in the natural sciences? Who knows? If not, then moral and scientific inquiry are on a par with one another. If scientific disagreements don't undermine the objective status of science, then moral disagreements shouldn't undermine the objective status of morality.

But what if this rosy prediction isn't realized? What if there is *still* a lot more ethical disagreement than scientific disagreement, even after all that tidying up is done? This isn't an idle question, unfortunately. There is a quite good reason for supposing that this is exactly what we should expect, even were we able to get more information, process it more effectively, become more imaginative, and correct for bias.

The reason is that scientific claims can be tested by **empirical** methods that scientists largely agree on. By contrast, there aren't any such methods for resolving ethical disputes. We can't touch or taste good and evil, can't easily quantify it and mathematically manipulate it, can't subject it to controlled experiments. It doesn't seem, when we are testing our ethical beliefs, that we are testing them against the world, in the way that we routinely do when investigating scientific claims. Since science is the model of objective inquiry, however, it appears that ethics, being so disanalogous, suffers by comparison. Science is objective. Ethics is different. Therefore ethics is not objective.

Now some will balk at that first claim. And the critics of science aren't entirely mistaken—clearly there are instances in which science (like the "racial science" practiced in Nazi Germany and apartheid South Africa) is really a play of political forces masquerading as a set of objective findings. Yet surely it overstates the case to suppose that the whole of science operates in such a way. We can grant that much of science is genuinely objective, and manages to describe a reality not of our own making, without committing ourselves to the false claim that the science of our day must have the final word about the nature of this reality.

If we assume that science does frequently manage to light on the truth, then we will want to know how ethics fares by comparison. And skeptics have a ready answer—not well. Scientists have hard data to confirm their claims. This data is a record of stuff we can see, or hear, or touch. We can quantify it and construct repeatable experiments to measure the accuracy of our predictions about it. It's tangible, material, and unquestionably real. Skeptical? Just step off that cliff or in front of that bus. Afraid? You'd better be.

But we can open our eyes, cock our ears, stick out our tongue, buy all the beakers and scales and lasers we want, and still, we won't be any farther on in verifying moral claims. This can be unsettling. Skeptics hope you'll think so. Though some philosophers deny it, there does seem to be a genuine contrast between the availability of empirical confirmation in science and the absence of anything like that in ethics. The question, of course, is what to make of this contrast. Skeptics claim it gives us all we need to vindicate skepticism. I don't think it gives us anything at all.

To see why, we need consider only this home truth: ethical inquiry is a form of philosophical inquiry. And philosophy is fundamentally different from the natural sciences. Therefore we should expect, and not be discouraged by, the crucial differences that exist between scientific and ethical investigation.

Ethics is a branch of philosophy. Everyone accepts that. Once we make this explicit, it should come as no surprise that there are intractable disputes within ethics. After all, there are intractable disputes within *every* branch of philosophy. Yet a moment's thought will show how implausible it is to suppose that these deep, persistent disagreements are evidence for a general philosophical skepticism, that is, a denial that there are objective truths within philosophy.

Consider just two of many possible examples to illustrate this point. Philosophers have differed for millennia over whether God exists. And there's every reason to think that philosophers will continue to disagree on this matter, for as long as our species is around to question such a thing. What follows? Nothing at all. In particular, it surely does not follow that there is no objective truth about God's existence. Either there is an all-perfect deity or there isn't. We may never know for sure. But clearly there is some truth of the matter, and just as surely, that truth doesn't differ from person to person, or society to society. *Beliefs* about the matter differ in this way, but not truth. It doesn't make sense to say that a perfect being exists for Smith, but not for Jones, unless it's just a roundabout way of saying that Smith does, and Jones doesn't, believe that such a being exists.

Perhaps another example will cement the point. Philosophers have long disagreed about whether there is such a thing as free will. When we think about our own choices, we seem, in almost every case, quite able to have chosen otherwise than we in fact did. Staying home or going to work, exercising or reading a book, pasta or rice—it's really up to us. We rarely have a gun to our head, literally or figuratively. When we don't, our decisions are ours to make. We have free will.

But we are also material beings, and so governed by natural laws that don't incorporate any exceptions for free will. Look in *Physical Review* or *Astrophysics Journal*—not much mention of free will in those pages. But if we are material things, constrained by natural laws, then all of our actions and choices are necessitated to occur as they do. And that leaves no room for free will. Alternatively, if we can somehow escape the confines of natural laws, then some of our doings are not necessitated. But then they are random, chance, fortuitous events. And if they are like that, then how could they possibly be free, ones for which we can be held morally responsible? Such actions are more like the erratic twitchings of a seizure victim, or the chaotic movement of subatomic particles, than anything over which we can be said to exercise free choice.

Either way we lose. If our actions are necessitated, then they can't be within our control. If our actions are not necessitated, then they are random, and, again, outside of our control. So our actions cannot be within our control. Therefore we have no free will.

I have just supplied the barest outline of a classic philosophical argument. It has worried thinkers for centuries. There is no agreement, to this day, on how to resolve the issues it raises. Yet certainly there is an objectively correct answer to the question of whether we have free will. Either we have it or we don't.

Whether we have free will doesn't depend on our opinion on the matter. I don't get free will just because I want it, or think I have it. And I don't get free will just because my culture says I do. Society doesn't have the final say on such matters. If it did, there would be no point, for instance, in a work such as *The Crime of Punishment*, written by a prominent psychiatrist, Karl Menninger, in the late 1960s. Menninger advocated the abolition of punishment precisely because we lack free will (or so he thought). And therefore we can never be truly blameworthy, which we must be if we are ever fit to be punished. Menninger may have been mistaken, but we can't prove that just by saying (correctly) that he was flying in the face of deeply held cultural beliefs about personal responsibility and accountability.

The point here isn't to try to resolve the free will debate, but rather to use it as an example to illustrate a crucial point. Philosophers, like scientists, proceed on the assumption that the goal of inquiry is the discovery of objective truth. It may not come in our lifetimes. There may never be unanimity or enduring cross-cultural consensus on philosophical matters. But that isn't enough—not nearly enough—to warrant the inference that takes us from the presence of intractable disagreement to the absence of objective truth.

Thus, intractable ethical disagreement fails to provide probative evidence for moral skepticism. For if it did, then we would have to abandon belief in all objective philosophical truth. But this is absurd—there is an objective truth about the existence of God, or free will, or the nature of ethics. Moral skeptics assume as much when they claim that, *objectively speaking*, good and evil are human constructs. Skeptics don't claim that their view is true only for them, or for those in their culture. They claim that there are no objective standards of good and evil, period.

Let's run that Argument from Disagreement again, only in a slightly modified version: If a claim is the subject of intractable dispute among thoughtful people, then it isn't objectively true. *Moral skepticism* is the subject of intractable dispute among thoughtful people. Therefore it isn't objectively true.

Hmmm. The present conclusion is logically entailed by the two premises. And the second premise is true—moral skepticism *is* the subject of intractable disagreement. So moral skeptics had better abandon that first claim. But once they do, the Argument from Disagreement crumbles, its crucial premise abandoned. And even if, perversely, skeptics cling to that first premise (thus undermining their own view), it is anyway false. All sorts of philosophical claims are subject to deep, persistent dispute. Yet some of them are true— objectively true. Intractable disagreement does not, after all, signal the absence of objective truth. If it did, there would be no objective philosophical truths. There are such truths. Therefore a claim, in- cluding (for all we know) many an ethical claim, can be objectively true even if it never attracts a consensus among well-informed, open- minded people. The fact that we can't agree about which ethical views are true and which false is sometimes disheartening. But it shouldn't sap our confidence that some such views really are true, regardless of what we (or others) think about them.[1]

---

[1] Skeptics might still insist that intractable disagreement prevents our ever gaining knowl- edge of these objective truths. And what good is objective truth if there's no way of dis- covering it? In Chapter 18, I try to show why pervasive disagreement is no obstacle to moral knowledge.

CHAPTER 15

Does Ethical Objectivity Require God?

Most people think that if moral rules are objective, then they must have been authored by God. This includes **theists**, many of whom believe in God precisely because they believe in ethical objectivity, and see no way of defending that idea without God. But it also includes all those **atheists** who embrace moral skepticism, just because they believe that the only escape from it is through God, whom they reject.

The *Argument from Atheism*° is the classic expression of this last line of thought. It's an extremely simple, powerful argument. It says that ethics is objective only if God exists. But God does not exist. Therefore ethics isn't objective.

It would be a lot of fun to talk about that second premise—the claim that God doesn't exist. But it would also take another book to do it justice. I can beg off that project for another reason as well, an even better one: we don't have to settle whether God exists in order to decide on the merits of ethical objectivism. Ethical objectivism can be true even if God doesn't exist.

To see how we can pull that rabbit out of a hat, let us reflect a bit about why so many people are convinced that what I have just said is false. In other words, consider why most people find the first premise of the Argument from Atheism so compelling: ethics is objective only if God exists. Why think that?

In my own experience, people tie objectivity to God because of a very specific line of thought. The basic idea is that all laws (rules, principles, standards, etc.) require a lawmaker. So if there are any moral laws, then these, too, require a lawmaker. But if these moral laws are objective, then the lawmaker can't be any one of us. That's just true by definition. Objectivity implies an independence from human opinion. Well, if objective moral rules aren't authored by any one of us, then who *did* make them up? Three guesses.

In a nutshell: all rules require an author. Objective rules can't be human creations. Therefore objective rules require a nonhuman creator. Enter God.

The basic problem with the Argument from Atheism is that both theists and atheists can (and should) reject it. It is obvious why theists will reject it. Its second premise is just an assertion of atheism. If you are convinced that God exists, then this Argument is a nonstarter for you.

You might be wrong, of course. It may be that God really does not exist. But unless the atheist can provide compelling argument to that effect, then you theists out there are within your rights to reject the Argument from Atheism. And agnostics are in pretty much the same boat. Agnostics are those who believe that the evidence for or against God's existence is evenly weighted. They suspend judgment on the question. If they do that, then they, too, will find the Argument from Atheism less than compelling. For they'll neither accept nor reject its second premise (the avowal of atheism), and so will refrain from endorsing its conclusion.

But what if you are an atheist? Why shouldn't you accept the Argument—after all, it's named in your honor! The answer is that you ought to reject the first premise of the Argument (the claim that ethical objectivity requires God). Why? Because the reasoning that supports this premise is one that atheists will not accept. Recall that the reasoning stipulated that laws require lawmakers, and that objective laws therefore required God. But atheists deny that God exists. So atheists must either reject the existence of any objective laws, or reject the claim that laws require lawmakers. Since they can easily accept the existence of at least some objective laws (e.g., of physics or chemistry) they should deny that laws require authors. But once we get rid of *that* view, then there is no reason at all to suppose that objective moral rules require God's existence.

Here's another way to look at the matter. If objective ethical rules require God, that's because (i) rules require authors; (ii) therefore *objective* rules require nonhuman authors; (iii) therefore objective *moral* rules require a nonhuman author; and (iv) that must be God. Each of these steps follows naturally from the preceding one. Atheists reject the conclusion (iv). Therefore they should reject the initial claim that got them there: (i).

If you are an atheist, you do, in fact, believe that all objective laws lack a divine author. As far as you can tell, such a being doesn't exist. And objective laws—of the sort we find in mathematics, or astronomy, or hydrology—are not of our own creation. We have identified them and given them names, but we have not invented the truths that they represent. So in these cases we have instances of laws without lawmakers. Who created the law of gravity? No one. Who made the second law of thermodynamics true? No one. If these laws are objective, then *we* certainly didn't create them. And if God doesn't exist, then, obviously, God didn't make them up, either. No one did.

Here's a reply you might be thinking of: while scientific laws may be authorless, **normative** laws—those that tell us what we *ought* to do, how we *should* behave—do require an author. So all of these scientific examples are besides the point. Even if we concede the existence of scientific laws without lawmakers, we still need some reason to think that moral laws, which are obviously normative, are also authorless.

I disagree. The best reason for thinking that moral laws require an author is that all laws require an author. But that reason, as we've seen, is mistaken. What other reason could there be?

I don't think there is one, or at least one that works. Not all normative laws require lawmakers. For instance, the laws of logic and rationality are normative. They tell us what we ought to do. But no one invented them. If you have excellent evidence for one claim, and this entails a second claim, then you *should* believe that second claim. If you are faced with contradictory propositions, and know that one of them is false, then you *must* accept the other. If you want just one thing out of life, then you *ought* to do what's necessary to achieve it.

None of these are moral principles. But they *are* normative ones. If you are an atheist, you'll deny that God made up such principles. If any principles are objective, these are. So we have here objective, authorless, normative laws. Objective principles, scientific or normative, need no authors.

What all of this means is that if you are an atheist, then you should reject the first premise of the Argument from Atheism. That premise—objective ethics requires God—appears plausible only because of a further view (laws require lawmakers) that you should not accept. If you believe in objective laws at all, then you will deny that they have authors—they just *are* true, period. You can take the laws of math, logic, and the natural sciences as models of those that are neither human nor divine artifacts. That doesn't prove that ethical laws are also objective. But it does show that God isn't necessary to establish the existence of objective laws in general. Scientific and normative laws might be objective even if God does not exist. If God is claimed to be specially necessary for moral laws in particular, that will require some further argument, something that has yet to make its appearance.

So whether you are a theist or an atheist, you should reject the Argument from Atheism. Atheists will reject its first premise, because they will be able to cite objective laws that do not require a divine author. And theists will reject its second premise, because it just begs the question against their view. The Argument has lost its constituency. Regardless of your take on religious matters, you should reject the Argument from Atheism.

Perhaps you never liked the Argument in the first place. Maybe you're a theist. And suppose you're right: God exists. Then it's easy, isn't it? If God exists, then God is the author of morality, and morality is objective. That is the most natural, straightforward way of getting God into the picture. But it is also deeply problematic. In fact, it turns out that even if you believe in God, you should have serious reservations about tying the objectivity of morality to God's existence.

One of the classic attributes of God is that of Author of morality. If, as most Western theists believe, God is the source of everything, then God must also be the source of morality. So when we ask the familiar question—where did the standards of right and wrong come from?—the answer, from a theistic perspective, is: God. God decides what is right and wrong. God communicated that information to us, in a working out of the divine plan. It is our job to do our part, and aspire to live in accordance with the divine decrees.

You've all heard that story before, regarding it, perhaps, as a pernicious fiction, or as a comfort in distress. Despite its familiar feel, the thinking it represents has been rejected by most philosophers who have thought about it, including most theistic philosophers. To see why is to see why ethical objectivists—even the theists among them—should insist on the existence of a realm of moral truths that have not been created by God.

The philosophical story begins almost 2,500 years ago. In one of Plato's early dialogues, a man named Euthyphro confidently tells Socrates of his impending lawsuit. When Socrates asks him who he is prosecuting, Euthyphro tells him that he is bringing his own father up on murder charges; he allowed a slave to die of exposure; this is murder, and piety requires a conviction. Before you know it, Socrates and Euthyphro are off, enmeshed in a discussion of the nature of piety that would have lasting repercussions in the history of Western thought.

Euthyphro is now remembered for the dilemma that Socrates sets the title character: is an action pious because the gods love it, or do the gods love it because it is pious? We can focus on rightness, rather than piety, and replace the polytheism with monotheism, to get the question that contemporary theists must face: is an act right because God loves it, or does God love it because it is right?

Many theists suppose that it would be somehow irreligious to embrace the dilemma's second horn. If God loves actions because they are right, then this seems to undermine God's omnipotence. For in that case, God is not the author of the moral law, but rather one who invariably knows how to appreciate it (namely, with love at the sight of virtue). If God loves actions because they are right, then it isn't God's love that *makes* them right. Actions would be right prior to, or at least independently of, God's love, which would be a response to a moral feature of the world that is already there. Divine love would not endow an action with its moral character; rather, such love would be an unerring response to the moral qualities that await divine appreciation.

This has the sound of heresy to some, precisely because it posits a moral law that exists independently of God's having created it. But even if you are a theist, you should take such an option seriously. For consider the alternative: acts are right because God loves or commands them. Now it is God's say-so that makes it so, transforming something that was previously morally neutral into something that is good or evil, right or wrong. This may sound very congenial. But it is actually a quite problematic picture of how God relates to morality.

If the objectivity of ethics hinges on God's existence, that must be because objective moral laws require a nonhuman author. The **Divine Command Theory** tells us that there is one, and so our qualms about moral skepticism can be laid to rest. This theory tells us that actions are right because (and only because) God commands them. But if a divine command lies at the heart of ethics, then ethics is arbitrary, an implausible collection of ungrounded moral rules.

How can that be? Surely God's commands are anything but arbitrary. Since these commands are said to be at the foundations of morality, the charge of arbitrariness must be mistaken. But it isn't. The picture offered by the Divine Command Theory is, to caricature it only a bit, one in which God awakes of a morning, yawns and stretches, decides to create a morality, and then picks a few dos and don'ts from column A and column B. Is there anything wrong with this picture? You bet. But this is the picture we are left with on the assumptions that drive the Divine Command Theory.

If God's say-so is what makes actions right or wrong, then we have to ask: does God command and love things for reasons, or just arbitrarily? If arbitrarily, then this is hardly a God worthy of worship. The caricature would be right in all essentials. God would be the inventor of the moral law, and so God's omnipotence wouldn't be threatened. But if there were nothing that *justified* God's commands, no reasons that compellingly supported a choice to prohibit, rather than license, killing, theft, perjury, etc., then these choices really would be baseless.

We might put it this way. Either there are or are not reasons that support God's commands. If there are not, then these commands are arbitrary, and so the foundations of morality, if created by God, are infected with this arbitrariness. Alternatively, God may have reasons for the divine commands. *But then these reasons, and not the commands themselves, are what justify the schedule of duties.* God's commands would not create the standards of good and evil; instead, they would codify the standards that are sustained by whatever reasons God has relied upon to support the divine choices.

Take a humdrum example to illustrate this point. Suppose I am appointed the referee at a sporting match. Imagine that one team has just scored, and the rules of the game dictate that the opposing team should now take possession of the ball. Suppose also that I follow the rule and give the ball to the opposing team. If I continually act like that, then I am a good referee. What does my goodness consist in? My unerringly following the rules. I don't make up new rules willy-nilly. I know all the rules and enforce them consistently. When I make a call, I can cite relevant reasons to justify it—pre-existing reasons, rather than ones I make up on the spot, with no rationale.

It may sound odd, or mildly blasphemous, to liken God to a sports referee. But I don't think there's much harm in it. The Divine Command Theory has us picture a God who controls our game in its entirety, making up all the rules, perhaps continually, and having no need to cite any reasons on their behalf. For what reasons could there be? If there are no moral rules or reasons prior to God's commands, then there is nothing God could rely on to justify the divine commands. So any choice is arbitrary. Had God woken up on the other side of the bed on that fateful morning, we'd be saddled with a morality that encourages torture, pederasty, perjury, and all sorts of other things we now recognize to be evil.

How could God possibly license such wicked deeds? Easily enough. If there wasn't anything wicked about them prior to God's decree—nothing intrinsically evil about such conduct—then God could just as easily, at the moment of decision, have gone one way rather than another. Does anybody really believe that? That a true, divine morality could just as well have allowed torture, rape, and assault as forbid such things?

No, you say, such a thing is impossible. A *good* God would never allow such a thing. Right enough. But what does it mean to be good? If the Divine Command Theory is correct, then something is good just in case it is favored by God. But then look what happens: to say that God is good is just to say that God is favored by God. Is that really what we mean when we say that God is good? Moreover, there is nothing about this characterization that ensures that such a self-loving Being wouldn't have chosen torture over compassion. To love or favor oneself is one thing. But there is no necessary connection between being a self-loving being, on the one hand, and prohibiting such things as torture and rape, on the other.

A good God, like a good referee, is one who plays by the rules. When we speak of God as morally good—indeed, as morally perfect—what we really mean is that God cannot fail to uphold and respect all *moral* rules. A perfect referee or judge is one who knows all of the relevant rules, doesn't make them up arbitrarily, and applies them in an exemplary way with an eye always toward making the game (or the trial) the best it can be. Perfect referees or judges are not authors of the laws they apply. They are not free to change them at will. Their worth, their goodness, is measured by the respect they display for the rules they are asked to enforce.

Change the relevant rules from those of games and trials, to those of morality; the analogy is otherwise very close. The rules that God enforces are moral rules. God knows them all. God enforces them all, with perfect justice. And God doesn't make them up arbitrarily. God's goodness consists not in divine authorship of the moral rules, but actually in a kind of divine limitation: God *cannot* do anything other than act in perfect conformity to morality, and cannot help but perfectly apply the moral rules to those creatures who are subject to them.

What theists mean when they say that a good God wouldn't command such a thing as torture is that *since torture is evil*, no one who is good could direct us to commit it. This makes perfect sense. But it also assumes that the moral character of torture (killing, rape, etc.) is fixed prior to God's reaction to it. And that means that God is not the author of the moral law.

In other words, we manage to preserve God's goodness only by instituting a picture of the origins of morality such that God, being omniscient, knows all facts—including all moral facts. And God, being all-loving, cares enough about us to impart some of that wisdom to us (in the form of your favorite scripture). This outlook preserves God's omniscience and perfect goodness. The cost: God's authorship of the moral law. God sees what is there to be seen—namely, that torture and rape are evil, and that compassion, kindliness, and bravery are virtues that we should all aspire to.

What this all means is that even theists should resist taking up the view that God is the author of the moral law. God is constrained by the moral laws, in the same way that God is constrained by the laws of logic. Most theologians do not take this logical constraint as any strike against divine omnipotence. On the contrary—such omnipotence is usually understood to mean that God can do anything at all *within the limits of logical possibility*. (God cannot, for instance, make contradictory claims simultaneously true.)

I am suggesting that theists amend this traditional view to say that God's omnipotence enables God to do anything, so long as it is compatible with the laws of logic *and* the laws of morality, neither of which are divinely created. Embracing that view allows theists to make excellent sense of the idea that God is perfectly good—God is the one who cannot fail to abide by all the laws of morality.

The bottom line here is that the best option for theists is to reject the Divine Command Theory, and so reject the idea that things are right just because God commands them. Instead, a perfectly good God would command actions because they are right. And that means that there can be an objective moral code that is not authored by God, but instead is recognized by God (being perfectly knowledgeable), imparted to us by God (being perfectly loving), and enforced by God (being perfectly just).

Of course, it might be true that God does not exist. But that would be no threat to ethical objectivism. According to atheists, there is no author of the universe, and so no author of the countless objective laws that govern it. Since authorless objective laws, on this account, pose no special problems, there is no bar to prospects of ethical laws that are also objective.

On the other hand, it might be true that God does exist. If so, then we have an obvious source of moral objectivity. Yet if I am right, we do well to resist this picture, and to accept the Socratic invitation to see actions as right prior to God's endorsement of them.

In short, there are three major options here, and *all* of them are compatible with the existence of objective ethical laws. First option: God doesn't exist. If that is so, there are still plenty of objective laws (of physics, mathematics, logic, genetics, etc.). Moral laws might make that list, too. Second option: God exists, and is the author of the moral law. Obviously, objective moral rules follow directly. Third option: God exists, and is not the author of the moral law, but rather perfectly knows, complies with, and enforces it. If my criticisms of the Divine Command Theory are on target, then this option is the preferable one for theists, and also carries with it the promise of objective ethical laws.

So whether you are a theist or an atheist, or still up in the air, ethics can be objective. Whether you like my criticisms of the Divine Command Theory or not, ethics can be objective. No matter God's role in morality—as Author, as perfect Enforcer, or as nonexistent fiction—ethics can be objective.

CHAPTER 16

Where Do Moral Standards Come From?

Much resistance to ethical objectivism stems from puzzlement about how there could be moral standards that are not human creations. If we don't fix the content of morality, then who does? The natural reply: God. But we have just seen reason to doubt that. Hence the $64,000 question: if God didn't make up the moral rules, and humans didn't make up the moral rules, then who did? Where do moral standards come from?

We have two options. If neither humans nor divine beings invent the moral rules, then perhaps someone else made them up. (Space aliens?) The other choice, one that I hope we are now accustomed to taking seriously, is that no one at all made up the moral rules. The question—who invented the moral law?—is operating under a false assumption. Not every law requires an author.

Admittedly, the claim that the moral rules were never invented by anyone is going to leave a lot of people with a bad taste in their mouth. And that's because that view seems to imply a further view that seems ridiculous. The further view is that the moral rules are eternally true. If no one made them up, then there was never a time when they just popped into existence. And if that is so, then they are eternal. Yet that is implausible. So the original claim, one that posits an authorless morality, is implausible as well.

Why are eternal moral truths thought to be illegitimate? Because such truths seem to commit us to the idea that there are moral facts that existed prior to the appearance of human beings. If moral truths predate the origins of humanity, then there was always such a thing as good and evil, even in the age of the dinosaurs. Many find such a view preposterous: moral standards apply to beings like us, so if we are gone from the scene, then so too are the moral standards that would govern our behavior.

So: an authorless morality is an eternal morality. An eternal morality is implausible. Thus an authorless morality is equally implausible. Recall modus tollens: if a claim implies a falsehood, then the original claim must be false as well.

There are two possible replies that objectivists can make, and I think that they can both succeed. The first is to deny that an authorless morality must be an eternal one. The second is to deny that there is anything absurd about a set of eternal moral truths.

First things first. Morality may lack an author without being eternal. There are familiar examples of objective laws that are not eternal—those regulating the workings of DNA, photosynthesis, and sedimentary compression, for instance. Prior to the existence of chromosomes, plants, or rocks, there were no laws of these kinds. The relevant laws came into being just at the point when these things assumed a nature capable of accurate description. Who authored those laws? No human being, certainly; indeed, humans didn't even exist at the time when such things first came into existence.

We can date the origin of natural laws to the origin of the things that such laws cover. Since organic matter, etc., has not existed eternally, neither do the natural laws that correctly describe their nature and behavior. Yet these natural laws are objective. So an objective law need not be eternal. If that is so in the natural world, then we will need a special argument for thinking that things are different in the moral world.

I don't know of any such argument. But suppose this is just ignorance on my part, and that we have to live with the claim that an objective morality must be an eternal one. This isn't as problematic as earlier examples made it seem.

How could morality be eternal if morality applies only to beings like us, who came into existence only a relatively short time ago?

The answer is found in a distinction: that between a moral principle and a moral fact.

What is a moral principle? It is, first and foremost, a conditional (an if-then claim). If certain conditions are met, then a certain moral verdict follows. For instance, a moral rule prohibiting killing says that *if* one kills, *then* one does wrong. All moral rules are like this. They specify conditions under which actions, motives, practices, etc., exhibit a particular moral quality.

Moral facts are not principles, but realizations of moral principles. A moral fact is an instance of goodness, or rightness, or virtue, etc. It is the bravery of a partisan in the Warsaw ghetto, the compassion of a teacher comforting a hurt child, the integrity of a civil disobedient taking the blows of a malicious police force.

The distinction between fact and principle is all we need to turn the criticism that an eternal morality has absurd implications. Certainly there can be no moral *facts* prior to the appearance of humans (or beings relevantly like us). Before we arose, there were no instances of moral goodness or evil, since there wasn't anyone around who could satisfy the conditions set forth in the moral principles.

But is it really so absurd to suppose that at least some of the moral principles themselves are eternal? *If* you torture another for fun, then that is wrong. This is true even if there are no people around to torture. It will continue to be true even after the human race is extinct. My hunch is that all of the deepest moral principles are like this.

Nor are such examples restricted to ethics. Consider a geometrical principle that specifies the properties of some nonexistent figure: *If* a figure is trillion-sided, two-dimensional, and equiangular, then _____. (You fill it out; I haven't a clue.) There's got to be some correct way to fill in that blank, even if no one presently knows how to do it. Whatever it is, the emerging principle will be true, even if there never was, and never will be, a trillion-sided figure of that description. Principles can be true even if they are *never* instantiated, that is, even if the conditions they set forth are never met.

So moral principles could be true even before humans were around to exemplify them, and even after they have perished one and all. Certain moral truths, such as those prohibiting torture and those enjoining aid to the vulnerable, could be true for all time.

There may be no *instances* of torture until humans enter the picture, and so no moral facts implicating its wrongness, but the principle that condemns such behavior would have been true prior to any of its instances.

For those who are still having trouble with such a thought, consider the case of mathematical principles. It always has been and always will be true that two and two are four. No one invented this rule, though certainly people invented the language to express it. Prior to the invention of language, no one could have said such a thing, or perhaps even thought it. But it was true anyway.

A billion years ago, two atoms combined with another two still made four atoms, though no one was around to name the fact. Does this strike you as odd? If so, it's probably because of a specific view about how facts relate to language. The view is that there can be no facts without language. But that view is false.

Imagine a world prior to the existence of any language. There actually was such a world—this one, for most of its existence. Imagine the world as it was half a billion years ago. Wasn't there something that the earth was like, way back then? Rocky in spots, marshy elsewhere, undersea in this region, etc. There were countless facts about the earth's nature, despite the absence of anyone who could have said what they were. Further, those facts would have remained facts even if human beings had never existed—even if there never were any beings capable of conceptualizing them and rendering them in language.

So there can be reality, facts, and truths even prior to the existence of human beings. And there can be truths—specifically, true principles—even if they are never exemplified. And so, for all that's been said, there can be moral principles that are true even prior to the existence of human beings, even after human beings have departed from the scene, and even if such principles are never exemplified.

Here's an example designed to cement those points. It isn't pretty. I propose that the following moral principle is eternally true: it is wrong to hammer nails into a living baby, chop it into a billion pieces, boil the remains, and force its mother to drink the concoction. Thank God such a thing has never happened. Hopefully it never will. Neither of these points alters the truth of the principle. Lest you think that such a principle comes into existence only when human babies do, imagine the scenario only slightly changed. Suppose, a thousand years from now, that we encounter beings just like us in every way, except that their sustaining systems are silicon-based, rather than DNA-based. Still, it would be wrong to mutilate and murder such a baby. The fact that such beings don't exist, and probably never will, doesn't alter the truth of the amended principle.

If you agree with that, then you have come around to the idea that moral principles might be eternal. For such principles can be true even if they are never exemplified (much like the principle about the trillion-sided figure). They can be true prior to the existence of the things they mention (the alien infanticide example). They can be true even prior to the existence of a language, or a language user, capable of formulating them (two atoms and two atoms . . .). Since that is so, what is to prevent us from saying that they were *always* true? For consider: if such principles are allowed to be true even prior to the existence of the things they mention, then at what earlier point did they become true? I don't see any nonarbitrary moment one could rely on. Short of that, it seems that they were always true.

Brief recap. The main criticism we are entertaining in this chapter is the one that charges ethical objectivists with an obscure account of the origins of moral truths. If moral skepticism is false, then moral principles are not human inventions. If the Divine Command Theory is false, then God doesn't make them up, either. No one else is left. So it must be that no one makes up the moral rules. But if that is so, then it seems that objectivists are committed to the existence of eternal moral truths, and that seemed very implausible.

My reply: first, an objective morality need not be an eternal one. Moral principles could be relevantly like those that govern DNA, photosynthesis, etc.—they came into being only when the things they describe took on a determinate nature. Yet I also bit the bullet, and in the last few pages have tried to show that the idea of eternal moral laws is not as weird or implausible as might have been thought.

Who makes up the moral rules? No one. Then where do they come from? Well, where do the laws of chemistry, or physics, or mathematics come from? It may sound lame to say that such laws come from the way the physical, or chemical, or mathematical world is ordered. It's not that illuminating an answer. But it does have the virtue of being true. And not every question admits of an illuminating answer. Likewise, when moral skeptics ask where moral truths come from, the answer needn't be: us. There are many reasons for thinking such an answer false. The answer just might be: moral truths come from moral principles, which themselves are true provided they correctly describe the nature of the moral world. That's hardly thrilling. But it may be all we can hope for from such a question, especially if, as I have argued, we cannot rely on human or divine opinion to fix the content of our moral principles.

CHAPTER 17

Values in a Scientific World

Good and evil are values. But what could a value be? It seems to be something unique, unlike anything else in the world. In an inventory of the world's contents—philosophers call this an **ontology**, a list or theory of what exists—will we really find anything that answers to our notions of good and evil?

Suppose, with objectivism, that moral judgments are true, and true quite independently of what we happen to think of them. They are true, when they are, because they accurately report objective moral facts. But the nature of such facts can appear very mysterious. We readily grant that geologists and chemists, physicists and astronomers deal in objective truth, because we believe that their findings are targeted on a natural world whose features exist independently of whether anyone recognizes them. Botanical facts are facts about plants; geological facts are facts about rocks. In botany and geology, evidence is supplied by three-dimensional, tangible, physical stuff. We can taste it, smell it, touch it, and see it. We can't taste wrongness or hear rightness. Moral facts, if they were to exist, would have to be quite odd sorts of things, certainly nothing at all like the kinds of phenomena studied by the recognized sciences.

Suppose we make an effort to understand the nature of objective reality, and are searching, in particular, for what exists prior to our contributions to the world. This ontology will surely include such things as molecules, stars, catfish, clouds, and atomic particles. It will include such features as having six sides, a symmetrical structure, or a hard surface, and being colorless, a foot long, a micron in width, and soluble in water. Is there any room in there for good and evil?

The basic reason for suspicion stems from an application of **Occam's razor**. William of Occam, a medieval philosopher, instructed us not to multiply entities (or suppositions) beyond necessity. If there are competing theories to explain some phenomenon, then the better theory is the one that makes the fewest assumptions, or posits the fewest mechanisms. His maxim, which is basically a counsel to adopt the simplest, most economical view of things, is almost universally embraced within philosophy, mathematics, and the natural sciences.

To see how Occam's razor works, consider one of its more famous applications: the vindication of the Copernican theory of planetary orbit. The Ptolemaic conception that it replaced was positively baroque by comparison. Copernicus explained the same phenomena that Ptolemy sought to, only with far fewer assumptions, positing far fewer entities. Conversion to the Copernican system didn't occur overnight. Conceptual revolutions rarely do. But its ultimate triumph lay primarily in its ability to explain all that Ptolemy's theory was able to do, with the added benefit of employing fewer assumptions into the bargain. Occam's razor at work.

We can deploy this stratagem in the service of a powerful *Argument from Occam's Razor*° against ethical objectivism. This argument asks us to survey the world and report on its contents. And it tells us to do so by employing the following test: is the thing in question required to help us to explain what we see in our world? If the answer is No, then we have reason to abandon any belief in it. And the moral skeptic claims that when we have a careful look at what surrounds us, we'll have no need of the objectivist's assumption that the world contains moral features.

To get a better sense of what is at stake here, consider what has happened to once-predominant views about the existence of God, or the immortal soul, or leprechauns and trolls. Though many still believe in God and the soul, why have we seen so great an increase in skepticism about their existence? Why have we seen the *complete* abandonment of belief in leprechauns and trolls? Doubtless there are a variety of cultural factors involved. But there is also, and perhaps primarily, a philosophical source of such doubt. That source is Occam's razor, and the eponymous Argument that gives expression to it.

Supernatural forces were once invoked to explain why regions suffered drought, why people died, why rivers ran their course, why volcanoes erupted. These explanations have been threatened by modern science. Since there is a scientific explanation for all of these happenings, what is left for God (or those other supernatural beings) to do?

We can put the question even more sharply. Consider any given event in the world—how about catching a cold? There is, it seems, a complete medical explanation for this occurrence. Perhaps no one has all of the details for any given case, but science tells us that, in principle, we could cite an extremely complex biochemical story that explains how a person (say) contracts influenza.

With this story in hand, what room is there for anything else to get into the picture? Knowing what we now know, we *need* to refer to microbes, immune systems, and viruses or bacteria in order to explain why people get sick. That's why we are justified in thinking that such things exist, even though we can't see them with the naked eye. But given that the biochemical story can offer us a complete picture of the origins of a cold, we haven't any need to go beyond its details. The reason we don't believe in leprechauns or trolls is that they don't explain anything. Everything they were once invoked to explain has been better, more efficiently explained by the workings of modern science.

In effect, what the moral skeptic is giving us is a universe exclusively regulated by scientific laws, containing only the things that are ratified by science. Ethical objectivists give us a fuller, more expansive ontology. This includes all that science does, but adds an additional layer—moral principles and facts. In addition to protons, neutrons, electrons, molecules, gases and liquids, we also get good and evil, virtue and vice. Skeptics wield the razor to pare away such superfluous things. All that needs explaining can be taken care of strictly within the scientific viewpoint.

When we ask what is in our world, where should we begin? It's natural to begin with what we can see. And we quickly move to what we can hear, and touch, taste, and smell. In short, we take in the evidence of the senses and then ask how they can be best explained. What in the world (literally) is causing us to have the experiences we do? When we find out what it is, we can add that to our ontological catalogue. And not before.

We are justified in thinking that there are trees, and buildings, and rocks, because if we walk long enough, we'll bump into them. We've got some evidence—a bruised shoulder, a bumped shin—and we need to account for it. And once our curiosity gets the best of us, we'll want to know what made the trees the way they are, what made our shins as vulnerable as they are, etc. In pursuit of such knowledge, we develop and apply ever finer instruments and hypotheses to account for the phenomena we are investigating. We've gotten all the way to nucleotides and string theory. Who knows where we'll end?

The question for ethics is whether or not all the evidence of our senses requires the postulation of moral facts to explain them. Do we need the categories of good and evil, of right and wrong, to explain how clouds form, why rainbows appear, why people succumb to disease? It doesn't seem so. In fact, it doesn't seem that moral qualities help to explain *anything* that occurs in the natural world. But then we have two choices: either they aren't needed to explain anything at all, in which case Occam's razor tells us that they don't really exist, or they *are* needed to explain something, but something that isn't part of the natural world.

There are problems either way we go. If moral facts explain nothing at all, then why believe that there are any such things? The best reason we have for discrediting belief in trolls and ghosts, after all, is that (i) we've never seen any such things, and (ii) these things aren't needed to explain anything we *have* seen. It seems that we can tell a perfectly parallel story in the case of morality.

Have you ever seen evil? You may think so. Perhaps only in films, if you're lucky. But what have you really seen? Two persons, perhaps, one with a rifle, hauling a child out of her home and pushing her to her knees. Soldiers nearby, laughing and encouraging their comrade. The one with the rifle casually lifts it to the chest of the little girl. You hear a noise. The girl falls in a heap. Blood leaks from her body. The soldiers move on, buoyant, looking for another victim.

If you've seen such a thing, you've seen evil—if that's not evil, what is? But you could provide a full description of all the actions of such a scene, and never once mention evil. You'd mention the position of the rifleman and his victim, the soldier's words, the way he manhandled his victim, her look of fear, the impact of the bullet, etc. You don't *need* to cite the evil of the action to completely explain what happened. All the explanatory work can be done without it. The girl didn't die because of evil—she died because of a bullet to the chest. You have to mention that to explain her death. You don't have to mention evil at all.

Because reference to the moral quality of the interaction is optional, it isn't required. And Occam's razor tells us that, therefore, we have no reason to believe that it's real. Moral skeptics capitalize on this and allege that either evil is nonexistent, or that evil is a human construct. There is no such thing as evil, really. If evil exists at all, it is only as a result of our projecting onto a value-free world our emotional repugnance at actions that, taken in themselves, are entirely morally neutral.

David Hume, the most brilliant of the philosophers of the Scottish enlightenment, captured this very idea more than two hundred years ago:

> Take any action allow'd to be vicious: Wilful murder, for instance. Examine it in all lights, and see if you can find that matter of fact, or real existence, which you call *vice*. In whichever way you take it, you find only certain passions, motives, volitions and thoughts. There is no other matter of fact in the case. The vice entirely escapes you, as long as you consider the object. You never can find it, till you turn your reflexion into your own breast, and find a sentiment of disapprobation, which arises in you, towards this action. . . . [W]hen you pronounce any action or character to be vicious, you mean nothing, but that from the constitution of your nature you have a feeling or sentiment of blame from the contemplation of it. (*Treatise of Human Nature*, Book III, Part I, Section I)

In a thorough description of all that the world contains, we will require no mention of virtue or vice. Even wilful murder, the epitome of vice, can be wholly described without the use of any moral vocabulary at all. Just the facts, ma'am. A coroner's report or a police blotter may include a full description of truly sociopathic behavior. But it needn't go on to register a moral verdict of the matter. That is gratuitous, at least from an explanatory standpoint. Adding the fact that the gunman's actions were depraved, evil, vicious, etc., tells us nothing we didn't already know about the cause of death.

So Occam's razor supports Hume's moral skepticism. Because we don't need to cite moral facts in order to explain the goings-on in the natural world, we have no reason to believe in them. There is the world that science tells us about. There are our emotional responses to that world (e.g., our "sentiments of disapprobation"). And that's it.

The alternative for the ethical objectivist is to claim that moral facts *are* needed to explain things, but things that lay outside the purview of the natural sciences. If moral facts really are explanatorily indispensable, then Occam's razor will insist that we keep them in our catalogue of the world's contents. But are they really indispensable in this way?

A problem arises when we ask, specifically, about what moral facts might be needed to explain. There are two possibilities: moral facts could explain nonmoral facts, or moral facts might explain other moral facts. The first option isn't promising. We have seen, in considering the wilful murder case, that moral facts (such as an agent's evil nature, or evil action) don't really add anything to an explanation of the nonmoral occurrences in the world. All that takes place in the natural world can be explained without citing the moral qualities of things.

So that leaves us with the second possibility—moral facts are needed to explain things, but only other moral facts. Hitler's callousness, depravity, and cruel indifference explain why he was evil, for instance. This is all right, as far as it goes. But it doesn't go very far, and that's putting it kindly. For the objectivist strategy here is really nothing other than a classic case of begging the question. You beg the question when you presuppose what must be proved. The present strategy is to defend the objective existence of moral facts by claiming that they pass the Occam's razor test. They are explanatorily indispensable. If that's so, then what are they required to explain? Other moral facts. But this just *assumes* that there are moral facts in need of explanation, and that is the very point at issue. Skeptics are in the business of challenging the existence of such facts. We can't just assume that they're there, and then go looking for what will explain them (other moral facts). That puts the cart before the horse.

Well, now we're in trouble. Morality is in real danger of being cut out of the ontological inventory. We said goodbye to trolls and mermaids and centaurs. We never laid eyes on them, and we didn't need to rely on them in order to explain anything in our experience. Perhaps we must take our leave of moral facts for the very same reasons.

There is only one way out, and that is the hard way. Ethical objectivists must reject the claim that something exists only if there is an explanatory need that it fulfills. Moral facts aren't necessary to explain anything. But they may exist for all that.

There are at least three arguments that objectivists can rely on to defend such a claim. The first tries to reveal the absurd implications of the skeptical position. The skeptic insists that something exists only if it is needed to explain what we experience. But, as it turns out, only a very few things are needed for such a task. According to the skeptic's own test, therefore, everything else is nonexistent.

Let's make this a little less mysterious. Recall Hume's example of wilful murder, and my gloss on it. I had said there that if we want to understand why the victim died, we *must* make reference to the bullet that killed her, whereas we needn't make any mention of the evil or wrongness involved. According to Occam's razor, that entitles us to believe that bullets really exist. And that moral facts don't.

But must we really make mention of bullets to explain the cause of death? Couldn't we do as well, or better, by citing the biochemistry that led to the death? Surely there is a biochemical story to tell about what occurred during the fateful moments of the shooting. If we had that in hand, then why bring in bullets (and blood, and cessation of breath, etc.)? We *could* mention such things, but we wouldn't *need* to. And that consigns such things as bullets to the ontological dustbin. They don't really exist.

There's a general point here: Occam's razor forces us to abandon belief in most things we think are real. There's nothing special about bullets. Cars, pumpkins, hammers, dishwashers . . . the list is endless. Though we often do cite such things in explaining what goes on in our world, we don't need to. We could just as well talk in terms of molecules or atoms. Likewise, though we often do invoke moral features to explain things in the world, Occam's razor tells us that we haven't any need of such things. Someone's goodness explains why she cared for that lost child. The chairman's integrity explains why he votes according to the rules, rather than rigging the ballot to suit his preferences. A state's iniquity explains why so many rebel against it. All of these seem like perfectly good explanations. But if we are to do away with moral features, because they aren't really needed to explain what occurs, then we should be equally prepared to do away with most things.

We have two choices. Each is based on the claim that there is a parity between moral features and most other features of the world. We either keep such things as bullets and hammers in our ontology, or we scrap them. If we keep them, then we keep the moral features, too. We can do that either by abandoning Occam's razor, or by sticking with it and finding a way to conclude that such things pass its test. Alternatively, we might stick with Occam's razor, and claim that it cuts moral features out of the ontology. They aren't needed to explain what happens in the world. But then we need to get rid of most of what we think is real, since bullets, etc., would also be unnecessary to do any explaining. (All references to such things could be replaced by references to molecules and atoms.) As long as you're prepared to accept the reality of dishwashers and hammers (and bullets and blood and . . .), then you should be prepared to accept the reality of good and evil.

Here is a second objectivist argument to show that moral facts can exist, even if they aren't needed to explain anything. The key claim here is that moral facts are a species of *normative fact*. Normative facts are those that tell us what we *ought* to do. Normative facts don't explain anything. Yet they exist for all that.

In my own opinion, moral facts are most similar to another kind of normative fact—epistemic facts. **Epistemic** facts concern what we ought to *believe*, provided that our beliefs are aimed at the truth. If you believe something on the basis of excellent evidence, and know that your belief entails another, then you *ought* to believe that further proposition. This is a true epistemic principle.

Moral facts, like epistemic ones, are normative. Their existence, if I am right, does not depend on our finding an explanatory need that they satisfy. Occam's razor is too strict a test for the existence of normative principles and facts.

Here is an epistemic fact: you ought to believe that two and two are four. What does this fact (i.e., the fact that you ought to believe this equation) explain? Nothing. But surely there are things that you ought to believe, and just as surely, you (or your culture) don't get to have the final say about every such matter. You *ought* to believe a whole host of things that you don't, or don't want, to believe. Many of these are things that your culture doesn't believe, and doesn't want you to believe, either. The scope of our epistemic duties is not limited by personal or cultural opinion. There really are such duties. And they don't explain a thing.

The parallel with morality should be clear. We have good reason to think that moral duties exist, and do not ultimately depend on personal or cultural ratification. Those reasons are largely negative (consisting of the criticisms of moral skepticism in Part 2) and partly positive (laid out earlier here in Part 3). The question is whether the force of that cumulative case can be overridden by morality's failure to pass some explanatory test.

I don't believe that the test can be that powerful. I don't mean to suggest for a moment that Occam's razor is useless. Rather, I think we should recognize its limits. It doesn't work when applied to the normative realm. When we consider all of our oughts—what we ought to do in order to believe the truth, or behave morally, or maximize our self-interest, etc.—then we will expect answers that, as it turns out, have no ability to explain the workings of the natural order. Our epistemic and moral duties cannot explain why chameleons change their color, why cyclones form, or why heat rises. They may exist for all that.

Surely there are certain things that you ought to believe. If all the evidence is staring you in the face, then there's something you ought to believe, even if it's easier, or psychologically more comforting, to put your head in the sand. If your second-grader comes home and tells you that six times six is thirty-five, then there's something else she ought to believe—no matter how stubbornly she resists your counsel. It's easy to multiply examples. The point is that we all agree that there are certain things that each of us ought to believe. You don't really suppose that every such duty is just a fiction, or merely a matter of conforming to your own standards, or those of your culture. There really are epistemic oughts, epistemic duties. And there are moral ones, too. This despite the fact that such normative truths fail to pull their weight in the network of explanations that tells us how the natural world operates.

If we think about it for a moment, this shouldn't be all that surprising. The kinds of principles that science vindicates are essentially *causal* and *predictive*. We are justified in believing in them because they accurately cite the causes of events and predict what is going to happen. Their explanatory power consists in precisely this ability. The law of gravity tells me that every time I drop my keys, they're going to fall to the ground. And they always do. We are justified in believing in a gravitational force just because it can explain so many things better than any competing hypothesis.

But moral rules are not like that. The rule enjoining us not to perjure ourselves is true even if it is honored only in the breach. Moral rules don't depend for their justification on an ability to predict what will happen. Moral principles aren't meant to describe what people do, or anticipate their actions, but rather to *prescribe* how they ought to behave. They don't cite the causes of outcomes, but rather indicate what sort of conduct would merit approval, or justify our gratitude, or legitimate some result. Science can't tell us such things.

So we are really faced with a choice. If we take up an exclusively scientific view of the world, then there is no room for normative principles and normative facts. But such things do exist. There are genuine reasons to believe things, and genuine moral reasons to do things. Science cannot verify the existence of such reasons, duties, or principles. But that only points to the limits of science, rather than to the limits of a credible ontology.

One final argument. Think of the big picture here. What kind of world view is being advanced by those who would do away with moral features? My hunch is that something like *the confirmation test* is what underlies so much suspicion about morality. The confirmation test says that a claim is true only if it is scientifically confirmable. Since we can't confirm moral claims scientifically, they aren't confirmable at all. And if they aren't scientifically confirmable, then we have no reason to think that any of them are true.

Importantly, the confirmation test *cannot* be true. And so there can be truths whose existence escapes scientific confirmation. If I am right, objective principles that state our moral obligations are such truths.

Why can't the confirmation test be true? Simple: if we suppose that the test is true, then it is self-refuting. If we correctly apply the test, then it turns out that the test itself flunks. It doesn't measure up to its own standards. So it must be false.

Here's the basic idea: if the confirmation test were true, then it would be an instance of a true claim that cannot be scientifically confirmed. Science is totally ill-equipped to render a verdict on the merits of the confirmation test. The discipline best suited to assessing that test is *philosophy*. And philosophical claims are not the sort that can be verified exclusively by scientific means. (More on this in Chapter 18.)

Since the confirmation test cannot be true, we needn't decide what is real and unreal just by reference to what science can tell us. Indeed, based on arguments that we have already seen, and some yet to come, we have excellent reason for thinking that there is more to the world than science can reveal. Among these extra ingredients are normative facts and principles. And foremost among these are moral duties and moral rules. The fact that science cannot tell us how to behave doesn't mean that we are free to do as we please. It just means that science can't tell us everything we need to know.

CHAPTER 18

Moral Knowledge I:
Four Skeptical Arguments

Surely one of the greatest obstacles to a belief in objective moral truths is our puzzlement at how we might gain knowledge of them. If you are like most people, you'll assume that you are imperfect, can make moral mistakes, and that some of the moral convictions you now hold are mistaken (though you aren't sure which). Wouldn't it be nice to discover a method to sort out the true beliefs from the false ones? The problem is that there doesn't seem to be any good way to do this.

To get knowledge in any area is to have, at the least, some beliefs about it that are both true *and* justified. True beliefs aren't good enough. They might be the result of guesswork, of dependence on unreliable sources, of misconstruing the evidence. We want true beliefs that are well supported. The problem, says the skeptic,[1] is that

---

[1] Skepticism, in this chapter and the next, refers to doubts about the possibility of moral knowledge, rather than to doubts about the existence of objective moral truth. There can be those who are skeptical in both ways, of course—nihilists who, since they reject the possibility of moral truth, also reject the possibility of moral knowledge. But one might reject nihilism, or be neutral about the existence or nature of moral truth, and nevertheless insist that even if there is any, we cannot know it. This latter sort of view is going to be the focus of this chapter and the next.

we can't have justified moral beliefs. Ever. And so moral knowledge is an impossibility.

There are five major arguments that skeptics offer to defeat our hopes of gaining moral knowledge. One of them—the *Regress Argument*°—is so difficult that I've devoted the following chapter to it alone. Here is a preview of the four more tractable ones, starting with the argument that presents the least difficulty to the defender of moral knowledge.

That would be the *Argument from Certainty*,° which relies on the impossibility of ever being certain about one's moral claims. Knowledge, it is thought, requires certainty. But certainty is unobtainable in ethics. So moral knowledge itself is impossible.

Why is moral certainty unobtainable? Simple: for any moral belief you hold, there will be someone who is informed and rational, and who will remain unconvinced to the bitter end. This is the second skeptical worry, expressed in the *Epistemic Argument from Disagreement*.° The existence of rational, informed people with views that are diametrically opposed to yours undermines any justification you have for your beliefs. And yet this is precisely the situation that holds for *all* of our ethical beliefs. Therefore we can have no justification for our moral outlooks. And without justification, there can be no knowledge.

The *Perspectival Argument*° begins with the assumption that there is no uniquely best perspective from which to make moral judgments. Once we grant that assumption, and make the further claim that justified belief can be had only when one has adopted the best perspective for viewing a matter, then we get the result that we cannot be justified in any of our moral beliefs. Hence moral knowledge is an impossibility.

The fourth worry, which serves as the basis for the *Argument from Inadequate Evidence*,° concerns the kind of evidence we can have in support of our moral judgments. We have a clear idea of what counts as evidence in all other areas we acknowledge to be objective. Botanists study plants; geologists study rock formations; hydrologists study water. We know such things exist because we can see them. Moral facts aren't like that. It seems that all the evidence we have for our moral beliefs is our feeling that they must be right.

But that is a notoriously shaky basis for knowledge. Since ethics can do no better, any claim to moral knowledge is equally shaky.

Let's take these criticisms in order. This has the virtue of bolstering the spirit, since the first argument, as it turns out, is also the easiest to handle. Having disposed of it, we can buck up our confidence and tackle those that are substantially more difficult.

The first argument claims that we can't have moral knowledge because we can't have moral certainty. How should we plead? Guilty. We can't have certainty in ethics. But we are facing trumped-up charges here. The claim that knowledge requires certainty is mistaken. Or, if it is correct, then we can know almost nothing at all.

Before we show this, it is important to get clear on a terminological point. Of course people can *feel* certain about their views on moral issues. They may be absolutely unwavering in their commitments, totally sure that, at least in some moral matters, they can't be mistaken. But this feeling is compatible with error—indeed, it must be, if there are people who feel equally strongly about such matters, and yet disagree. They can't both be right. (That would be a contradiction.) So a feeling of certainty isn't the same thing as genuine certainty. Genuine certainty, like knowledge, entails that the proposition you are certain of is true.

Genuine certainty is almost nonexistent. Philosophy students learn this when they encounter René Descartes's *Meditations* for the first time. In his classic work, Descartes decides to cast aside all of his beliefs, in the hopes of starting with a clean slate. Only those beliefs that are literally indubitable—incapable of being doubted—will be retained, in order to serve as foundations for a reconstructed, pure edifice of knowledge. Every new belief will be either indubitable itself, or derived by pure logic from indubitable beliefs, so as to ensure the security of the entire network of beliefs. A classic philosophical dream. Everything is guaranteed, every belief underwritten by certainty and logic. Like many a beautiful dream, it was never destined to be realized.

To purge himself of possibly false beliefs, Descartes imagined an evil demon, who was manipulating him into thinking his present thoughts. He believed he was sitting before a fire, watching a candle burn. But he might have been dreaming. He was sure that two and three are five, but the certitude he felt at such a thought may have been just a manufactured confidence, implanted by an evil genius bent on deception. The basic problem is this: all the evidence that Descartes used to justify his beliefs (namely, other beliefs and experiences) could be equally explained on the assumption that an evil demon was deceiving him. Until he could eliminate that assumption, he couldn't be sure that his beliefs were true. And absent such certainty, he couldn't *know* whether they were true or false.

OK, not everything can be subject to this sort of sweeping doubt. In particular, Descartes came upon his famous maxim, *cogito ergo sum:* I think, therefore I am. So long as he was thinking—even thinking that he might be systematically deceived—there was someone doing the thinking. And so he could at least be certain of *that*. As it turns out, Descartes couldn't be sure of any other aspect of his own biography, for any such impressions might have been implanted in him by the evil demon. But he *could* be sure that so long as he was thinking, then there was something, he knew not what, that was doing the thinking.

And what else could he know? Just about nothing. Descartes himself supposed that he could, in the end, be confident about most of what he believed. But that was because he thought he could logically demonstrate God's existence. God, being perfect, could not tolerate systematic deception of the creatures that He lovingly created. So God wouldn't allow the sort of evil demon whose job it was to so grossly mislead Descartes (or anyone else). And therefore the initial credence that Descartes placed in most of his beliefs was warranted after all.

Descartes thought that from absolutely indubitable premises, he could, via perfectly logical steps, prove that God exists. Almost no one (other than Descartes himself) was convinced of his success. That was disastrous. Without God as guarantor of our beliefs, we are stuck with only those that are indubitable, or can be derived via pure logic from indubitable beliefs. And those are very very few. You think you are reading this now? You might be mistaken. You think you're living in the twenty-first century? (Possibly) wrong again. You think you know what town you're in, what the names of your family and friends are, what teacher you had in the third grade? Think again. You can't be certain of any of it.

You might be dreaming right now. Didn't you ever dream that you were awake, thankful that, at least this time, you weren't dreaming your good luck? Didn't you ever wish, within a dream, that it were only a dream, "knowing" all the while that it was an awful reality you had to go and face? If this has never happened to you, try a contemporary spin on Descartes's fantasy for a moment. It might be the case that, right at this very moment, you are just a brain in a vat, your cerebral cortex being manipulated by ingenious neuroscientists to simulate the activity of reading a book entitled *Whatever Happened to Good and Evil?* Can you prove that this is *not* what is happening to you? How would you do such a thing? All the evidence you bring forward is compatible with both hypotheses—the one that says you're a real, live person, just as you think you are, and the other, which says that, as a perfectly manipulated brain in a vat, even the appearances of your protesting your full-bodied existence are being fed into your cortex by the neuroscientists who control the brain that you are.

Here's a distressing bit of news. Philosophers have never solved this problem. They have never demonstrated the existence of an external world—a world that exists outside of your thoughts, a world whose details are mirrored in your thoughts, a world of 3-D stuff that exists independently of you. We all believe that there is such a world. And none of us can prove it.

What follows? Just this. If you insist on certainty as a precondition of knowledge, then you can know almost nothing. You can know that you exist, so long as you are thinking, though you can't know anything much about yourself. You can also know that things appear to you in certain ways—you can be certain that there *seems* to be a page here, right in front of your nose, that there *appears* to be a sun and a moon and other people about. Of that you can be sure. But you can't be sure that there *really is* a page here, a sun, a moon, and other people. You can't be sure that there is anything outside of you, and you can't even be certain about who you are—what your history is, what you look like, when you are living, etc. You could be dreaming. Or systematically deceived. You can't prove that you're not.

So here is the choice. Insist on certainty, and foreclose the chance of getting any real knowledge. Or relax the standards required for gaining knowledge. This latter is what almost every philosopher has done. Philosophers have taken from Descartes precisely the opposite message that he intended to convey: *don't* insist on certainty as a requirement for knowledge. It sets the bar too high.

If we can have knowledge without certainty, then, for all we've said so far, we might have *moral* knowledge without certainty. It would be unfair to hold morality to standards higher than those in any other area. Certainty promises a kind of epistemic purity. But it is a false promise, holding out hopes that can never be realized. If knowledge requires certainty, then we must abandon hopes for moral knowledge. But then we must give up on every other kind of knowledge as well.

Rather than do that, let's take up the second skeptical criticism, which tries to show that there is something especially troublesome about *moral* knowledge. Here, in the *Epistemic Argument from Disagreement*, we confront a variation on a familiar theme, one that seeks to undermine objectivism by pointing to the greater lack of consensus within ethics, as opposed to that found within the natural sciences and mathematics. Here the claim is *not* that intractable disagreement reveals an absence of objective ethical truth. Rather, the claim is that such disagreement undercuts the possibility of ever knowing what it is.

The basic idea is that persistent disagreement, at least among those who know all the relevant facts and are thinking them through efficiently, defeats the justification you might otherwise have for your beliefs. If you can't convince such a person, then maybe you shouldn't be convinced yourself. Though that sounds pretty plausible, there are two problems with it, one in practice, one in theory.

The practical problem is that you can never really be sure whether you have reached a point where an opponent's intransigence is reason for you to withdraw your endorsement of some moral belief. After all, he might not really have all the information he claims to have. He might be making some error of reasoning that isn't obvious in the heat of debate, or even after, in a cool moment of reflection. He might be failing to imaginatively place himself in some relevant position. He might be advancing a view that isn't really as coherent as he makes it out to be. These sorts of failings are often extremely hard to detect. So, in practice, just because another smart person morally disagrees with you, doesn't mean that his view is as well honed as yours. The disagreement itself isn't enough to force you to give up your beliefs.

We can reach the same result in theory as in practice. Suppose now that you are faced with an opponent whose moral views *are* as integrated, informed, and reasonable as your own. You certainly aren't required to go over to his side—remember, he's in the same position, and it would be odd were you two simply forced to switch belief systems. Rather, the thought must be that you are both required to suspend judgment about the controversial issue.

But if you are, then you're in trouble (and so are the rest of us). You will have to abandon just about every belief you presently hold. Every belief about the external world, for instance, must go. For there is a very sophisticated, internally consistent, well-informed position that tells us that if we can't discount the possibility of an evil demon, then we cannot know whether there is an external world. This was Descartes's position. You may not like it (neither do I), but that doesn't prove that it's wrong.

The bottom line is that for just about any belief at all, there will be detractors who are very smart, well informed, possessed of consistent views, and imaginatively flexible. If you think that any party to such a debate ought to suspend judgment, then you ought to suspend judgment about nearly everything. Brilliant skeptics have doubted the existence of an external world. Nothing you could say would convince them. Therefore (if the Epistemic Argument from Disagreement works) you must abandon belief in an external world. Do you really believe that?

If you're willing to bite that bullet, there's nothing I could do to convince you that moral disagreements aren't epistemically crippling. Instead, we have a dilemma. You choose the least painful option. Either intractable disagreement among consistent, intelligent parties forces them to suspend judgment about their contested views, or it doesn't. If it does, then we must suspend judgment about *all* of our philosophical views, as well as our belief that there is an external world, that I am an embodied being, that the earth is older than a second, etc. All of these have been challenged by brilliant, consistent, informed skeptics over the millennia.

Alternatively, if we are warranted in any of our beliefs, despite the presence of such skepticism, then justified belief is possible, even in the face of persistent disagreement. And so we could retain our moral beliefs, especially those that we have carefully thought through, despite an inability to convince all of our intelligent opponents. Take your pick.

The *Perspectival Argument* represents another familiar challenge to the possibility of acquiring moral knowledge. The argument says, in effect, that gaining knowledge requires us to occupy a special vantage point. But, in ethics, there is no special vantage point—no best perspective from which to render moral judgments. And, absent that best perspective, there is no basis for knowing whether any given moral belief is true or not.

Consider a simple analogy. Suppose you are an insurance investigator, looking into the causes of an accident. You get a number of different stories from the eyewitnesses. When that happens, you (rightly) trust the account of the person who was best situated to view the accident. One person had the best perspective. That is the person who knows what really happened.

The skeptic says that there's nothing like this in ethics; no best perspective from which to assess competing moral claims. But without that sort of privileged point of view, we are just seeing things through our limited, parochial, lenses. Such vision is cloudy and unreliable. It can't give us knowledge.

There are two ways to reply to this kind of argument. The first defends the claim that there really is a best perspective on moral matters. The second allows that there may be no such vantage point, but then says that such a perspective isn't needed for knowledge.

There is a lot of controversy about the first strategy. Many philosophers have tried to identify the elements of this preferred standpoint. One familiar try is given by a variation on the Golden Rule. To know whether an act is right or wrong, you need only ask: would you like it if that were done to you? If you would, then your act is right. If you wouldn't, then your act is wrong. But this often fails as a good standpoint. The sadomasochist wouldn't mind being hit, hard. But that doesn't make it right for him to go hitting others.

Another familiar picture of the ideal moral perspective is one in which a person is purged of his false beliefs, knows all of the relevant nonmoral information, has no personal interest in the matter at hand, and is impartial in his concern for others. The thought is that anyone who manages to occupy such an exalted position will have knowledge of what is right and wrong—her opinions, if formed under these conditions, can't be mistaken.

Philosophers call people who satisfy all of these conditions "ideal observers." Though this has been, historically, a popular option for specifying a moral vantage point, it remains a controversial position. In fact, there are three standard criticisms of ideal observer theories. First, many think that it's impossible for any of us mere mortals to become an ideal observer. No one can be perfectly impartial, be rid of all of her false beliefs, etc. So even if this is the morally best perspective, no one can ever occupy it.

Second, many think that this isn't, in fact, the morally best perspective. Some think that the best moral decisions are made from an engaged, passionate standpoint, rather than a neutral, detached one. Others think that impartiality isn't always a good thing, that it's sometimes morally advisable to give preference to parents, children, and spouses over others who are equally needy, talented, deserving, etc.

Third, many allege that the ideal observers will disagree with one another. And if they do, then contradiction ensues. And any theory that generates a contradiction is false. So the ideal observer theory is false.

Why would ideal observers disagree with one another (if they would)? Well, imagine a scenario where ideal observers consider the case of a woman seeking an abortion. Each observer, being ideal, is purged of all false beliefs. And each knows all there is to know about embryology, and the facts of the woman's situation. Neither observer has any special attachment to the woman. Both are relevantly impartial. Still, mightn't these two disagree about whether she should have the abortion? Most have thought such disagreement possible.

But being ideal entails knowing what's right and wrong. And knowing something entails its truth. So one ideal observer knows that the woman should have an abortion. And the other knows that she shouldn't. It follows that she both should and shouldn't have that abortion. And that's a contradiction.

Now it's important to note that the Golden Rule position, and the ideal observer strategy, are but two in a long line of attempts to discover a uniquely best perspective from which to make moral judgments. We can't investigate all such efforts. Instead, let's content ourselves with a couple of points.

First, despite the controversy that attaches to each such effort, there might, after all, be a morally best perspective. For instance, some version of the ideal observer view might be correct after all. To give us what we needed, it would have to be a version that was humanly achievable, one that gave us moral advice that we found deeply satisfying, and that ensured unanimity among ideal observers. *Perhaps* such a thing is impossible. Yet skeptics haven't given a decisive argument for thinking it so.

But suppose they do. Suppose there is no morally ideal perspective. It doesn't follow that we can't have moral knowledge. For there might be a number of quite good moral viewpoints, a number of strategies for obtaining moral knowledge, even if there isn't a perfect one. Utilizing one of these strategies, we might often gain moral knowledge, even if we don't always do so. We might know many things, even if we can't know them all.

To make this plausible, consider other areas where you think that knowledge is obtainable. If you're a moral skeptic, for instance, then you think that philosophy is one such area. By your lights, we can know at least this philosophical claim: that moral skepticism is true. But no one, to my knowledge, has offered any remotely plausible view of a uniquely best perspective from which to do philosophy. Of course, that might just be ignorance on my part. But if it is, then we've got just as much reason to suppose that there is a uniquely best moral perspective, since any "best" philosophical viewpoint is going to be at least as controversial as a similar one for ethics.

And matters don't end here. Physicists and biologists are in the same boat. There is no uniquely best vantage point from which to do physics, or biology (or economics, or chemistry, etc.). Scientists arrive at their results by means of different methods. They approach their subjects from different angles, some more intuitively, others more analytically, for example. Some view the world as if there must be some simple design underlying its complex manifestations; others are more comfortable accepting complexity at face value. There is no one thing properly called "the scientific method," or, if there is, it is sketched at a such a high level of generality (test hypotheses, gather evidence, use your senses) that many people, employing this same method, will arrive at contradictory results. And there is also no uniquely best manual for experimental design, which is a central element in scientific discovery. Instead, there are a variety of experimental paths to gaining knowledge in any given scientific field.

Try it for yourself: one is best poised to gain knowledge in _____ (fill in your favorite area of inquiry) just in case one meets these conditions: _____ (fill 'em in). If those who meet these conditions are allowed to make mistakes in their given field, then the chances that we can fill in the blanks for ethics rise a good deal. If those who meet these conditions can never be wrong, then the chance that the conditions can really be specified, for any area of inquiry, go way, way down.

I am in fact quite sympathetic to the idea that there is no uniquely best perspective from which to gain moral knowledge. But I could be wrong about that. And even if I am right, such a perspective isn't needed for moral knowledge. For it isn't needed elsewhere. On the assumption that we actually can have knowledge in other fields, we must ask whether there is any decent specification of an optimal vantage point for getting it. And there doesn't seem to be. So we may have moral knowledge after all, even if there is no uniquely best perspective that guarantees us access to it.

The last argument of this chapter concerns the kind of evidence that is available to defend one's moral views. The *Argument from Inadequate Evidence* claims that moral evidence is inferior to the evidence relied upon in recognized objective disciplines, because moral evidence is intangible and not quantifiable. Really, all the ethical evidence we can muster amounts to a recitation of our already-held opinions. And the fact that we hold a given view is no indication of its truth.

I think we must admit that ethical evidence is different in kind from the sort we find in the natural sciences. Provided we are entitled to trust our senses, scientists can rely on them to supply evidence to test a wide array of hypotheses. Ethics cannot rely on sense evidence in the same way, for any moral theory is perfectly compatible with such evidence. That is just a result of the observation that moral principles are not in the business of describing the natural world, or predicting its occurrences, but rather in evaluating it and telling us how we ought to conduct ourselves within it.

Our senses can tell us what is actually happening in the world. But they can't tell us what *ought* to happen in the world. All the empirical evidence there is leaves all the important ethical questions quite open. Two embryologists may know all there is to know about fetal development, and all there is to know about a woman's circumstances, and yet, consistently, come to absolutely opposed views about the morality of her intended abortion. True, our experience of the world may tell us what is impossible for us to achieve, and so it may, in that respect, narrow the moral options (provided that we aren't obligated to do the impossible). But that still leaves a huge variety of moral alternatives, each of which is perfectly compatible with all the empirical evidence there is.

If we can't rely exclusively (or even primarily) on empirical evidence to fix the content of our moral principles, then how can we justify our moral commitments? The answer comes when we recall the place of ethics in the larger scheme of things. Ethics is a branch of philosophy. We can't settle the debate about God's existence, or that of free will, or the nature of ethics, just by paying a visit to the Physics or Chemistry department and consulting their journals. Knowledge of moral standards, like philosophical knowledge quite generally, is not attainable solely by relying on the evidence and methods of science.

Unsurprisingly, philosophers disagree amongst themselves about how to discover and confirm philosophical truths. The reason is that this question is itself a philosophical one, and can be expected to be as controversial as most philosophical questions (i.e., very). There is intractable disagreement within philosophy about all of its major assumptions. As we have seen, this isn't enough to show that there isn't any objective philosophical truth.

But the question before us is not about whether there is such truth, but about whether we can ever retrieve it. In particular, we must ask whether the absence of determinative empirical evidence must cripple our hopes of gaining ethical knowledge. Since, it seems to me, that is just a more specific version of the general question as applied to philosophical knowledge, we won't get very far without tackling that last question.

If we wanted to find out whether there really was such a thing as (say) free will, what would we have to do? Well, a number of things. First, we'd have to get clear about precisely what we mean when we use the term. Then we would have to get all the relevant facts under our belt. We would solicit the views of those whose opinions we trust. We'd have to engage with the best of our critics to see whether we could answer their challenges, and whether they could answer ours. We must test our claims for logical consistency, and decide, in the face of contradiction, which of our competing views is least well supported. And we must investigate to see whether ours, among competitors, best exemplifies a host of theoretical virtues—economy, stability across cases, avoidance of ad hoc assumptions, preservation of existing beliefs, explanatory breadth, etc.

Every single stage of this process is fraught with controversy, since all but the second primarily involves philosophical exploration. The meaning of free will is itself a contested issue within philosophical circles. The appraisal of a critic's challenges is no less a philosophical task. The logical consistency of one's views isn't always transparent. The comparative assessment of whether one view best exemplifies a theoretical virtue is not to be resolved by appealing just to the evidence of the senses. We might as well face it. There is no way to pursue the philosophical method, as described in the previous paragraph, and expect that all of its intelligent practitioners will come to agreement at the end of the day.

In working through the method, we are prevented from relying primarily on empirical evidence to direct our findings. We must instead rely on our own considered views, as they emerge from this extensive battery of tests. This is what critics object to when they claim that, in ethics, the only evidence for our views is how we feel about things. We can now see that this is only a caricature of the philosophical method. The evidence we have is that of logical consistency, a check against recognized theoretical virtues, trial by fire in the face of criticism, and an obligation to defend, via argument, the claims that we believe to be true. All of this evidence is more controversial, typically, than that relied upon by natural scientists. But that, by itself, can't be a knock-down objection against the possibility of moral knowledge, since any claim to philosophical knowledge will be equally controversial.

The major lesson is this. If there can be philosophical knowledge at all, then it will not come primarily through empirical evidence, but via the **a priori** application of the philosophical method. The routes we traced a few paragraphs back will result in great controversy, but the existence of even intractable disagreement is not enough to undermine possibilities of philosophical truth or philosophical knowledge.

And, to get right down to it, doesn't everyone really believe that there can be philosophical knowledge? Those who doubt the existence of objective moral truths are taking a philosophical stance. If there is no philosophical knowledge, then either there is no philosophical truth, or there are no justified philosophical beliefs. But there are philosophical truths, and there are justified philosophical beliefs. So there is philosophical knowledge.

There is philosophical truth—it is true that God exists (or does not exist). It is true that we have free will (or true that we lack it). It is true that knowledge requires true belief. It is true that we have a soul (or true that we don't).

And everyone, even a moral skeptic, assumes that at least some of our philosophical beliefs are justified. Skeptics assume, for instance, that their own philosophical views, which deny the existence of moral truth or moral knowledge, are themselves justified. If such skeptical views, being philosophical, are not justified, then we needn't pay much attention to them!

As we saw in Part 2, those who are party to ethical and other philosophical disagreements all go on as if they were trying to discover the Truth, and, if confident about their views, proceed as if they were justified in asserting them. We may be mistaken. It is possible that there is no justification for any single philosophical or ethical view. But that, surely, is the position of last resort, and is belied by everyone who ventures an opinion in ethics, or philosophy generally.

If the sort of evidence we rely on to establish our moral claims is thought to be, by its nature, insufficient to justify our moral beliefs, then all philosophical justification must be discredited, since the pursuit of ethical truth exactly mirrors that of philosophical truth. Are any of your own philosophical views justified? You have opinions about whether God exists, about whether we have free will, about whether scientific reality is all the reality there is. You have beliefs about the morality of abortion, capital punishment, euthanasia, pacifism, and slavery. Are *any* of these beliefs justified? Don't you think so? (If you don't, why continue to hold them?) If any are, then there must be a way to justify them. However that is done, ethics can avail itself of precisely the same method.

If you abandon hope for moral knowledge, because you can't conceive of plausible evidence that can support moral claims, then you must also abandon all hope for philosophical knowledge. The very same kind of evidence, and the very same method of verification, are found for philosophy generally, and ethics in particular. This shouldn't be surprising, since ethics is, after all, a branch of philosophy. Both ethics, and philosophy generally, rely on considered judgments that are not primarily a matter of marshaling empirical evidence. Both proceed to confirm their claims by means of the a priori method described a few pages above. If there's no good evidence for ethical judgments, then there's no good evidence for any philosophical judgments.

We are now in a position to see why there must be good evidence to support our moral views. Remember modus tollens? If one claim implies another, and this second one is false, then the original one must be false, too. Well, here's one claim:

(E) There's no adequate evidence for moral judgments.

If (E) is true, then so is:

(P) There's no adequate evidence for philosophical views.

But (P) isn't true. Since that's so, then the original claim that implies it, (E), isn't true, either. And if (E) is false, then there is, after all, adequate evidence for moral judgments. In short, if (E) is true, then (P) is true. (P) is false. Therefore (E) is false. If there's no adequate evidence for moral claims, then there's no such evidence for philosophical claims. But philosophical claims can be well supported. Therefore moral claims can be, too. Modus tollens.

Who says that (P) is false—that philosophical claims can be well supported? You do. You have some philosophical beliefs, don't you? That God does (or does not) exist. That some people do evil and deserve punishment (or that everyone is a product of conditioning, and so should be immune from punishment). That morality is all a human construct (or something objective). That you can (or cannot) know that you are not presently dreaming. We all operate on the assumption that our philosophical beliefs are justified, even if we admit, as we should, that we aren't certain of their truth. But if any of these beliefs are justified, then (P) is false. And if (P) is false, so is (E). And if (E) is false, then there is adequate evidence for moral judgments.

Here is another way to show that (P) isn't plausible. A dilemma: (P) is either supported by evidence or it isn't. If it isn't, then forget about it. But what if (P) *is* supported by evidence? Then (P) is self-refuting! For (P) is a philosophical claim. (What else could it be?) If there is evidence to support it, then it can't be true. So either way—whether (P) is or isn't supported by evidence—we do best to reject (P). In rejecting it, we admit that there's good evidence to support philosophical claims. And if there is this good evidence, then there is also good evidence to support moral claims, which are, after all, a kind of philosophical claim. Moral knowledge is a real possibility.

In brief: if moral knowledge requires certainty, widespread consensus, a uniquely best perspective, or determinative empirical evidence for its support, then we can have no moral knowledge. But we can do without certainty. We can do without consensus. We can do without a best perspective. And we can do without determinative empirical support. We may have moral knowledge after all. ⭐

CHAPTER 19

Moral Knowledge II:
The Regress Argument

Here's an absolute classic. It's been around as long as philosophers have been thinking about the problem of how to gain knowledge, moral or nonmoral. It's called *The Regress Argument*, named after one of its especially problematic implications.

The difficulty stems from the apparent fact that every single moral belief can be legitimately challenged. And answering such a challenge seems to entangle us in a never-ending series of questions and answers. The infinite regress that results, like all infinite regresses, ends up justifying nothing. Since all of our efforts at moral justification are destined to result in such infinite regresses, there is no hope that our moral beliefs will ever enjoy any credibility. With that hope goes all hope of moral knowledge.

That's the argument in a nutshell. Now let's take things a bit more slowly. The argument begins with what seems an obvious truth: for any moral belief, we can always ask for its credentials. Supplying them requires citation of some other belief to back up the original one. Yet this further belief will itself require justification, and so on, and so on. In the real world, these question-and-answer sessions always come to an end. Yet that's just because one of the parties gets puzzled, frustrated, or exhausted. But what if we had infinite patience and infinite intelligence? Wouldn't the session go on *forever*?

It seems so. Yet this would result in a situation in which the chain of justification never stops—an infinite regress. And infinite regresses justify nothing.

The skeptic's claim is that all moral justification is subject to this problem, and that this undermines the possibility of justified moral beliefs. And in the absence of any such beliefs, there can be no moral knowledge, justification being a precondition of knowledge.

Anyone with a two- or three-year-old at home knows the problem. You tell her something, and she asks "Why?". You give her an answer, and she repeats the question. In fact, if you didn't just call a halt to the proceedings, she might still be asking you that very same question. "Because" probably didn't satisfy, but you exerted your authority and that was that. The problem is that in ethics, you can't solve problems just by asserting your authority. If someone is pesky enough to just keep asking "Why?", you owe him an explanation. The thought is that, in principle, such a line of questioning might never end. And until you can legitimately put an end to the questioning, none of the answers you give along the way will have a solid foundation. But you can *never* put a legitimate end to the questioning, since *every* moral claim can be plausibly challenged. Without an end to the questioning, we have no ultimate source of authority for our moral views. Therefore we can have no moral knowledge.

Here are the steps that get us to this disturbing conclusion. First comes the claim that all moral beliefs require justification. This is just another way of saying that each and every moral claim can be legitimately queried—we can always sensibly ask why it is thought to be true. A second claim says that justifying a moral belief is a matter of providing a reason for it, and any reason we give will take the form of some other belief. Now, third, these other beliefs, obviously, will be either moral or nonmoral beliefs. But, fourth, these other beliefs cannot be moral ones, and they cannot be nonmoral ones. Conclusion: there can be no justification for our moral beliefs.

Obviously, we need to know what's going on in that fourth premise. Just why are moral beliefs unable to receive justification from other beliefs? Let's first have a look at why *nonmoral* beliefs are thought to be incapable of justifying moral beliefs. The inspiration for that thought comes from a familiar source—David Hume. Hume famously wrote:

> In every system of morality, which I have hitherto met with, I have
> always remark'd, that the author proceeds for some time in the
> ordinary way of reasoning, and establishes the being of a God, or
> makes observations concerning human affairs; when of a sudden I am
> surpriz'd to find, that instead of the usual copulations of propositions,
> *is*, and *is not*, I meet with no proposition that is not connected with an
> *ought*, or an *ought not*. This change is imperceptible; but is, however,
> of the last consequence. For as this *ought*, or *ought not*, expresses
> some new relation or affirmation, 'tis necessary that it shou'd be
> observ'd and explain'd; and at the same time that a reason should be
> given, for what seems altogether inconceivable, how this new relation
> can be a deduction from others, which are entirely different from it.
> (*Treatise of Human Nature*, Book III, Part I, Section I)

Hume is telling us that we cannot derive an ought from an is, a pre-
scription from a description. What is the case is one thing. What
ought to be the case is quite another. One implication of this is that
there is a conceptual distinction between explanation and justification. We can always ask why any given act occurred, where we are
looking to explain a person's motives and the means she undertook
to achieve her goals. But we can also ask whether she was justified
in doing as she did. We should not confuse the two. In the context
of recent terrorist bombings, for instance, many supposed that citing the terrorists' motives and purposes entailed an endorsement of
them. But to explain their behavior is not the same thing as con-
doning it. It is not true that to understand is necessarily to pardon.

If Hume is right, then we can explain such acts as the destruction of the World Trade Center without being forced to justify (or
condemn) it. Whatever description you offer of the happenings in
the world, you are always logically free to select *any* moral evalua-
tion in response. You can't deduce an ought from an is.

What this means is that we cannot conclude a line of moral questioning with a nonmoral response. If you want to know why something is moral or immoral, citing some fact about the world cannot
serve as an answer. Take a case that's as morally uncontroversial as
they come: killing healthy little children is wrong. Suppose someone
asks us to defend such a view. Here are some familiar answers: killing
children is wrong (i) because it is taking life, or (ii) because I said
so, or (iii) because my society says so, or (iv) because that will diminish happiness in the world, or (v) because that would be breaking the law. If Hume is right, we don't need to get into the details

of these proposals, because they are all mistaken from the start. For any of these answers, we can always say, "Yes, I know that killing children is taking a life, will diminish happiness, is illegal, etc. But what's wrong with *that*?" These answers, and others like them, all assume that we can close a moral question just by citing some fact about the world. That, claims Hume, is an impossibility.

The alternative is to cite some further *moral* claim that can justify the one under scrutiny. So, for instance, if you want to know why it is wrong to kill little children, you might say that it is always wrong to kill human beings, or wrong to kill except in self-defense, or wrong to destroy the happiness of others, etc. On the surface, these sorts of replies are at least headed in the right direction. We may take issue with their details, but we recognize that they are the kind of reply we're looking for. The problem, however, is that any moral principle that could justify the prohibition on child killing will itself require justification. And then we have to ask how that supporting moral principle is itself going to be justified. If Hume is right, it can't be by means of some nonmoral belief. So another, further moral claim must be introduced, which itself will require justification via another moral belief, and so on, and so on.

The worry at this point is that the cycle of justification is unending. And without a final terminus, there can be no justification. Any given moral belief will require justification, and both possibilities for such justification (other nonmoral or moral beliefs) are unable to perform the necessary service. So there can be no moral justification. And therefore no moral knowledge.

There are four possible avenues of escape. First, we might reject Hume's insistence on the division between is and ought, and so end the moral questioning by positing some nonmoral fact. Second, we might claim that if the original moral belief derives support from enough other beliefs, and in turn provides them with some support, then the resulting overall coherence is enough to justify the moral belief in question. Third, we might end the regress by citing some self-evident, intrinsically plausible belief. And, fourth, we might justify the original moral belief by pointing out that it was very reliably formed. Let's take these in order.

The first strategy rejects Hume's credo and so claims that, in some cases, a statement of fact is sufficient to entail a moral conclusion. But this doesn't seem very plausible. For consider the most egregious case you can think of: a man batters his child—to death, and only because the child didn't clean up her room as she was told to do. Does this logically entail any moral conclusion? I don't think so. Those who note such a beating but fail to think it wrong are not illogical, but immoral. It certainly is immoral to do what this father has done. But we can't establish that point as a matter of pure logic. The inhuman monster who applauds the father needn't be contradicting himself. He is just grossly, perversely, immoral. He is right to note that this description of the father's conduct, like all descriptions, does not logically entail any moral conclusion. He is wrong—morally, not logically wrong—to draw the moral conclusion he does.

If what this father has done is immoral, then it follows that there is a moral principle prohibiting such behavior. We can say, for example, that the reason the father did wrong is that if a father kills his child for disobedience, then that is immoral. Notice, now, that our justification for the initial moral verdict is this moral principle—the conditional of the previous sentence. Perhaps every justification of a moral verdict will take this form (i.e., reliance on a supporting moral principle). But then how can we avoid the infinite regress? How can supporting moral principles themselves receive justification?

The second route claims that moral beliefs must be justified via other beliefs which, in turn, must themselves be justified. How are they justified? By being linked with yet further beliefs, *including the original belief in question.* Belief A is justified because it derives support from beliefs B, C, D, and E. How are these beliefs justified? They derive support from F, G, H, *and* A. Belief A receives its justification from, and in turn helps to justify, other beliefs. This is known to philosophers as the **coherence theory**, because it claims that a belief is justified in virtue of its cohering with other beliefs one holds. So long as you've got a tightly knit, internally consistent set of beliefs, each one deriving support from others, and in turn conferring support on still others, you've got the best possible justification for your views.

The problem for this view, one that its supporters have thought surmountable, is that it condones circular reasoning. Circular reasoning occurs when you use the view to be defended to help defend itself. For any belief, A, one can justify it by citing belief B. B is, in turn, justified by C. And C is justified by A. That's a pretty small circle, and obviously justifies nothing. Coherentists claim, however, that if the circle is sufficiently large, then this really isn't a problem. Opponents are unimpressed. A circle is a circle is a circle. And circles, they say, justify nothing, no matter their size.

There are those who advocate a different strategy. This begins with a challenge to a central assumption of the Regress Argument: the assumption that any justification for a belief must come from *other beliefs*. The first two strategies took this for granted. What happens if we give it up?

Historically, the most popular move to make here is to claim that certain moral beliefs, especially those that can serve to stop the regress, can justify themselves. They don't need any other beliefs for support. Some principles are so intrinsically plausible as to be **self-evident**. A belief is self-evident just in case one's understanding of it is sufficient to justify belief in it. If you ask me, for instance, what justifies my claim that nothing can be wholly a cube and a sphere at the same time, it wouldn't be amiss for me simply to reassert my view and put a stop to the questioning. What we have here is a self-evident belief—once you adequately understand its content, you just see its truth. We can't offer anything more basic than that, but we don't need to. Here is a belief that needs no further support.

Are there any moral beliefs like this? That's the question, and many have returned a negative answer. The allegedly self-evident principles of one age have turned out to be the rejected conventions of another. It is agreed by all that self-evident principles would, if they existed, be enough to stop the regress. But confidence in the existence of such principles has greatly dwindled, for many of the same reasons that explain the contemporary increase in moral skepticism.

My own view is that there are such principles, and that these can, therefore, do the necessary work to end an otherwise interminable line of moral questioning. The problem is that citing a moral principle as self-evident is bound to be more controversial than citing the principle (e.g.) about spheres and cubes. But controversy, as you now know, is overrated in my book. It doesn't show the absence of truth. It doesn't undermine justification. And it doesn't, or needn't, at least, always defeat a claim of self-evidence.

That is just assertion, not argument, and I don't expect anyone to just take my word for it. Rather than try to defend this line, which would be a very large task, let us instead move on to the final strategy for answering the Regress Argument.

The last strategy says that we cannot stop the regress by citation of nonmoral beliefs. We can't stop it through circular reasoning. We can't stop it via self-evident moral principles. In short, we can't stop it by invoking beliefs, either moral or nonmoral, self-evident or not. So how *can* we stop it? By looking at a belief's pedigree. According to this last strategy, a belief can be justified provided that it has emerged as a result of a reliable process. The fact that a belief has arisen in a particular way is what justifies it. So long as moral beliefs are reliably produced—so long, for instance, as the thinking and emotional processes that went into the origin of the belief are usually on track—then the emerging belief is one that we are warranted in holding.

On this line, there can be justified moral beliefs, so long as there are reliable belief-forming processes for them. And there very probably are. So long as there is truth in ethics, there are probably some pretty good paths to getting it, even if, at present, we are not certain of what they are.

The interesting part of this strategy is that a moral belief can be credible even if it isn't self-evident, and even if we don't have any other belief to back it up. We may draw a blank at defending ourselves in certain contexts—it may be, for instance, that when someone challenges you to defend your view that killing for fun is wrong, or that giving to others without thought of personal gain is right, you are just mute. You've got nothing to say. Some will claim that such principles are just self-evident. But the challenger certainly won't. He might be wrong, of course—he may just fail to see what is there to be seen. But if you don't like that idea, this fourth option gives you an alternative. It might be that these beliefs are justified even if you can't say anything on their behalf. They might be justified precisely because you came upon them in a good way—thought about things imaginatively, with attentive care and empathy, got the relevant information, etc.

I think that this last idea has a lot going for it, but, again, all I can do is record my sympathies with such a program.[1] What I wanted

---

[1] I discuss the attractions of the self-evidence and reliability options at much greater length in Part Five of *Moral Realism* (Oxford: Oxford University Press, 2003). Many other topics discussed in this book get fuller treatment there, as well.

to do was to show you that philosophers themselves have not abandoned hope in the face of the Regress Argument, and have developed a number of research strategies for fending off its skeptical conclusion. Rather than pursue any of these strategies in detail, which has been well and fully done in professional philosophy books and journals, let me conclude with a more general reply to the Regress Argument that seems to me to work.

If the Regress Argument destroys hopes for moral knowledge, it will have similarly disastrous results for knowledge of all kinds. If certain moral truths are not self-evident—if you're willing to doubt, for instance, even the claim that genocide is immoral—then why suppose that any nonmoral truths will be self-evident? If appeals to coherence in ethics are just covert ways to paper over a debilitating kind of circular reasoning, then justifying our empirical claims by appeals to coherence will be similarly ineffective. If having been reliably produced is not, after all, any help to the moralist seeking justified beliefs, then it won't be of any assistance in justifying our empirical or philosophical beliefs, either.

This is not news to philosophers. They are familiar with a version of the Regress Argument that was first made famous by Sextus Empiricus, a Greek philosopher who lived almost two thousand years ago. He claimed that every belief required justification; that justification had to come either from self-evidence, circular reasoning (coherence), or an infinite regress; that all of these options failed; and that therefore *no* belief was justified. Sextus deployed this argument as a way to undermine *all* knowledge, not just that in ethics.

If we can't use reliability, coherence, or self-evidence to distinguish the true from the false, then there's little chance that we can answer the Regress Argument. Perhaps we can't. But for those who are happy with this conclusion in ethics, beware—you can't be selective in your application of the argument. It's all or nothing. If you want to give up hopes of moral knowledge, there's a price—giving up on all knowledge. As a professor of mine once said: Believe it if you can.

CHAPTER 20

Why Be Moral?

About 2,400 years ago, Plato wrote his magnum opus, *Republic*, whose early sections contain a simple story. It is the tale of Gyges, a Lydian shepherd who happens upon a magic ring. Putting it on, he notices that when he gives it a half-turn, he becomes invisible. If you had such a ring, what would you do? Gyges knew at once. He immediately set out to kill the king, sleep with the queen, and take for himself the great stores in the king's treasury. He could act with impunity, and did.

Most philosophers nowadays believe that if there really were no chance that a modern-day Gyges would suffer jail time or assassination by assuming such absolute power, then it would be perfectly rational of him to do exactly as he pleased. The only reason for curbing our lustful, avaricious, competitive desires is that we may suffer for them in the end. If no such suffering is in the offing, then give them free reign. It's the rational thing to do.

The basic idea behind this view is that what it is rational for us to do depends entirely on what we want out of life. A person's rationality is entirely a matter of satisfying her desires and advancing her interests. In particular, there can be no reason for you to undertake a sacrifice, or forgo indulging your desires, unless there is the promise of gaining some greater good in the long run. Philosophers call this idea **rational egoism**, and I'll stick to that tag in what follows.

One of the key implications of this view is that any reason we have to be moral will be only **contingent**. That an action is cruel, ignoble, or vicious isn't, by itself, any reason to refrain. The only reason to refrain is that doing so will get you what you want in the end.

Will it? That depends. It's one thing to talk about each and every action, and wonder whether you'll always gain by behaving morally. If we're instead talking about how to live a life, about the sort of character one should try to develop, then morality may have quite a lot going for it. Looked at impartially, it may be that a virtuous person stands a better chance of living a happier life than a vicious one. Suppose you have a choice between raising a child along the path of virtue, or training him to be a person comfortable with deception and coercion. Suppose also that your choice was determined only by a concern for his well-being. Such a concern might dictate a virtuous life, even though, in some particular instances, he'd do better for himself were he to behave immorally.

Of course, this sort of moralistic optimism may be misplaced. There are times in which the virtuous are the first to die. If all of your reasons ultimately stem from your own concerns; if you are living in a time in which you are forced to choose between life and duty; if you are more concerned with living than with being virtuous, then you may be better off being an immoral person.

Chances that this is so only increase if we are asking, not about what sort of person we should be, but rather whether, at every opportunity, we have reason to choose morality over immorality. It has struck many as simple common sense to assume that doing one's duty will, in some instances, only undermine one's happiness and frustrate one's desires.

If that is true, and if rational egoism is true, then, in those circumstances, we will have no reason to do as morality dictates. We will have reason to be moral only when it suits us—only when there is something in it for us. On such a view, morality has no independent authority over us. If all our reasons derive from our own concerns, then, if morality conflicts with these, so much the worse for morality. Those who are most secure in their power, and also most evil in the exercise of it, would have no reason at all to change course. Morality's authority would thus be wholly contingent, depending entirely on whether our ends happen to align with its edicts.

This view may be true, though I certainly hope it isn't. And I am not alone—it has been the fond hope of many to be able to convict the villainous not only of immorality, but of irrationality: if only we could get Gyges and his lot to *see reason*, then they would come around and behave themselves. But if they haven't any reason to change their ways, no reason to treat their vulnerable subjects any differently, then we cannot appeal to their reason in pleading for their kindness. All we can do is to try to trick them into being moral (thereby acting against their interests, and so irrationally), or take up arms. It isn't a pleasant choice.

Of course, most thinkers who embrace this view about reasons try to soften its implications. They claim that tyrants and evildoers really always do have reason to be moral, since their harmful actions may come back to haunt them. If they would take a sufficiently long view of things, they would see that doing good is always the best policy.

But that can sound naive, at best, and fatuous at worst. Isn't it just unwarranted optimism to suppose that one's deepest desires will always be best satisfied by doing good? That virtue will always be rewarded? Many a tyrant has died peacefully in his sleep, at the end of a life filled with pleasures.

So far we haven't made any mention of how ethical objectivism might enter this discussion. It's now time to do that, in a way that brings out the skeptical implications of what has been said. *The Argument from Rationality*° opens with a dilemma: either there always is, or there sometimes isn't, good reason to do as morality says. Most of us are crossing our fingers and rooting for the first option. I know I am. But at what cost?

The argument that describes this cost is difficult, perhaps the trickiest that we've yet encountered. In broadest outline, its lesson is that if one endorses ethical objectivism, one must give up the ancient hope of showing that everyone has reason to behave morally. Objectivists can't have their cake and eat it, too. Most of us, most of the time, will have reason to be moral. But objectivists can't make this an ironclad guarantee. If you're in the market for such assurance, best to abandon ethical objectivism.

The argument has five steps. The first is to assume (just for purposes of argument) that we all do have reason to be moral. The second is a statement of rational egoism: we have a reason to do something only if it will serve our ends. (When I speak of *ends*, I'm referring to our wants, goals, and interests.) From these two claims we get a preliminary conclusion: we morally must do something only if it will serve our ends. Add one last claim: you alone get to fix your own ends. It's a subjective matter. It follows from all of this that what you are morally required to do is also a subjective matter, depending very importantly on personal choice. And that is directly incompatible with ethical objectivism.

So, if you want to ensure the rationality of being moral, as the first premise claims, then you pay the price. The only way we can ensure that we have reason to be moral is if morality is fixed by reference to personal choices. So either we always do have reason to be moral, in which case morality is subjective, or morality is objective, in which case we sometimes lack any reason to be moral.

Some objectivists bite the bullet. They say it's just a hard truth we have to live with—people's reasons stem from their own goals, morality doesn't always further these, therefore people don't always have reason to be moral. For instance, people might be so depraved, and so secure in their depravity, that they really don't have any reason to do what morality tells them to do. On this account, our moral duties are objective, but our reasons are subjective. Our reasons are determined by our ends; our moral duties are determined independently of such things; therefore we don't necessarily have reason to do our duty.

This is, in fact, the most common response to the Argument from Rationality. But it isn't the only one, and, by my lights, it isn't the best one. To appreciate the options here, let's start at the other end of the spectrum, with the skeptic's reply. Skeptics may actually agree that we all *do* have reason to be moral. But that would be because, as they see it, both morality and rationality are subjective. Nothing here is objective. Our moral duties are determined by us, and so are our reasons. The perfect coincidence of duty and reason explains why it is always rational to do one's duty: our duties, like our reasons, are determined entirely by the ends we select for ourselves.

There are two options for those who find such a view too slack, and yet hold out hopes of vindicating both objectivism and the rationality of moral conduct. The first way, the one that Plato himself advanced, rejects the fourth premise of the Argument. That premise, recall, says that our true ends are fixed by personal decision. Plato rejected this. He argued that we each live best, in the sense of doing what is best for ourselves, when we act virtuously. You don't think so? You're wrong.

Who are you to decide what's valuable—even for yourself? You're no philosopher. (Plato was unashamedly elitist.) Most people don't know what is good for them. They let their desires and emotions govern their choices, rather than letting reason decide what is right and good. They live foolishly, mistaking appearance for reality, the worthless trappings of the material world for true goodness.

According to Plato, each of us, depending on our capacity to be governed by reason, has a set of purposes that we are best suited to achieving. These purposes determine our interests. We don't get to set the purposes—that is an objective matter. So we don't get to fix our interests, either—that, too, is an objective matter. Whether you know it or not, or like it or not, your ends are fixed independently of your say-so. And, as it turns out (again according to Plato), those purposes perfectly correspond with the requirements of virtue. Thus it is always rational to be virtuous.

Though I would like to think that Plato was right about virtue always serving self-interest, in my heart of hearts I can't really bring myself around. It does seem that the greater part, perhaps the entirety, of settling my interests is *up to me*. My choices determine my good. I get to decide whether leaving philosophy, or having children, or learning Urdu, is good for me. And, to get directly to the point, how many of us have made our own moral perfection our ultimate goal? If we are the arbiters of what truly matters for our lives to go well, then morality coincides with self-interest only to the extent that morality helps us get what we want, or is regarded as important in its own right. Morality will fail to play that role for some people, at some times. In those cases, morality and self-interest will work at cross purposes, rather than in harmony. Virtue won't always serve our wants and interests. Thus if reasons stem exclusively from personal choice, we won't always have reason to be moral.

I don't have anything like a knock-down argument against Plato's claim that morality and self-interest perfectly coincide. It would be lovely were it true. I simply register my doubts about it, doubts shared by most contemporary thinkers. Of course, receiving such endorsement is no guarantee of truth. Indeed, I think that the central error of the Argument from Rationality is its second premise, rational egoism, which is accepted by most philosophers nowadays as the correct theory of reasons.

Rational egoism tells us that a person's reasons are wholly dependent on what matters to her. I think that this is false. Sometimes, for instance, we have a reason to help others just because they need it, even if providing such help is no part of our plans; indeed, even if it interferes with what we want most. We'll get no compensation for such assistance? We have reason to help anyway. We'll be late for that crucial interview? Tough luck.

If a person is drowning before your very eyes, and you can easily save her, then that's what you've got to do. Your inconvenience doesn't alter your obligation. Nor does it extinguish your reason to aid the person whose life is in your hands. You don't want to help her out. There's nothing in it for you. But surely there is *some* reason to help, isn't there?

Rational egoism says that there may be no such reason, even in these circumstances. It all depends on what you care about. But why make the existence of reasons depend just on that factor? Reasons are those considerations that favor or oppose, justify or condemn, some course of conduct. Why think that all such *normative* considerations depend on our personal choices? In fact, we have already seen a great many arguments to oppose such a conclusion.

Rational egoism suffers from the very same flaws as its moral cousin, ethical egoism. **Ethical egoism** claims that there is just a single, ultimate moral duty—to look out for Number One. Anything else is immoral. Strange as it might at first appear, the fatal flaw of such a view is that it amounts to a kind of unjustified discrimination. It requires you, systematically, to give favor to one person (yourself) over all others. That sort of extreme partiality calls out for justification.

Some discrimination *is* justified. I give some of my students A's, others B's, etc. This is a policy of preferential treatment—some are getting better rewards than others. But this is all aboveboard, because in this case I do have a plausible justification—some, on the basis of their work, deserve a higher grade than others. But ethical egoists don't have any such rationale. In a conflict of interests, why do I, from a moral point of view, *always* get to treat myself as more important? There's no good answer to that question. Not that I always must give you, or anyone else, priority. Sometimes neither of us should receive preferential treatment. Sometimes I get it, sometimes you; it all depends on morally relevant features of the case. What's most implausible is the thought that my self-interest is the *only* morally relevant consideration there is.

The very same problem affects rational egoism. Why think that the only legitimate reason I can have is to serve my own ends? Why, from a rational point of view, am I the only one who counts? As far as I can tell, there is no good answer to that question, either.

Someone is in danger of imminent harm—we have some reason to save him, especially if we can do so at only minimal risk and cost to ourselves. Someone has just fulfilled her end of the bargain, and now desperately needs you to do the same. In circumstances where nothing has changed since the deal was made, you certainly have some reason to keep your word, even if you can get away with breaking it. A man takes a fancy to another woman, walks out on his family and doesn't look back, leaving his wife and children in dire poverty. He has reason to contribute to their support, even if all he feels at the moment is contempt for his wife's situation, and nothing at all for his children.

Though rational egoism may sound fine in the abstract, when it comes to cases, we all reveal a commitment to its rejection. We can have a reason to do something, even if there's no chance of it doing us any good. And if that is so, then we may, after all, have reason to do our duty, even if morality's counsel doesn't always neatly align with our concerns.

So: why should I be moral? When people ask themselves this question, they are almost always faced with a situation in which being moral is going to cost them. And they want to know why they should go ahead and take the hit. But the British philosopher H. A. Prichard noted almost a century ago that there's really no good answer to this question. Not because we all lack reason to be moral. But because of the peculiarity of the question itself.

Prichard realized something that might sound picayune, but is really of the first importance. Take a look at the question again: why should I be moral? How do you understand that simple word, *should?* If I should do something, that means that I have excellent reason to do it, or that I am obligated to do it. But Prichard claimed that all of our reasons and obligations exist only within some framework of rules—those of morality, the law, self-interest, etc. So, in asking why I should be moral, I must really be asking whether I should, from a moral point of view, or a legal framework, or a self-interested perspective, do what morality says. And then the question is easy.

From a moral viewpoint, certainly I (morally) should do what morality tells me to do. That's pretty clear. But it's always an open question whether, from the perspective of the law or self-interest, I should do what morality tells me to do. The demands of the law, as we all know, never perfectly coincide with those of morality. And though we can hope for a close connection between morality and self-interest, there do seem to be times and circumstances in which the two pull apart.

This is Prichard's lesson: if you are intent on finding a reason to be moral from outside of morality, then the game is over before it's begun. Morality's authority will be only contingent, and your reason to be morally obedient will depend entirely on whether the law, or self-interest, coincides with morality's demands. In bad times it won't.

Of course, *if* you care about morality, then you will certainly have reason to follow its demands. But in that, the moral law would be no different from the by-laws of a fife and drum corp: an optional set of rules that bind you only so long as you continue to enjoy and participate in that way of life. Tired of drumming? Opt out. You're not rationally required to maintain your membership. Tired of being a morally upright person? Opt out. The moral rules are no more rationally compelling than the by-laws that regulate your marching steps.

Can you really just kiss morality goodbye like that? I don't think so. Of course you can revoke your pledge of allegiance (if you ever made one). But it doesn't follow that you are rational to do so, even if you are faced with a case in which doing your duty comes at your expense. If rational egoism is false, as it seems to be, then what reasons you have do not depend entirely on your choices, your inclinations, interests, desires, or goals. You don't have the final say about the content of your reasons—some of them (not all of them) are objectively fixed.

Some of these reasons are epistemic ones. Whether you like it or not, if you believe that it will either rain or it won't, and also believe that it won't, then you'd better believe that it will. You have a reason to believe this, even if you don't recognize it. Even if you disavow it. You just do.

Moral reasons, I would argue, are also like this. Sometimes we fail to appreciate them. Sometimes, when brought to our attention, we refuse to recognize them. There are moments when our sights are so limited that we cannot appreciate their existence and their power. That an act is cruel, pitiless, atrocious, or morally criminal is by itself reason to refrain. Some will not see this. That doesn't mean that they are automatically let off the hook. It means instead that there is such a thing as moral blindness, which encompasses not only ignorance about the content of morality, but also indifference to its authority.

CONCLUSION

The paces we've been put through here are typical of philosophical conversation. At the end of the day there is still plenty of ground to cover, plenty of questions to ask, and numerous criticisms to level. I'll leave these last for you. No doubt you've found, as all who do philosophy do find, that many of the views you have read and thought about are deserving of more criticism than an author realizes. That is all part of the philosophical enterprise. It would be small-minded of me, after having leveled so many of my own criticisms, to suppose that the views entered here will escape untouched. But if I am right, there is an excellent explanation for this: there is truth in and about ethics, and a truth that exists independently of my belief that it does. Our job is to find it.

I won't bore you with a recitation of the points I hope to have scored against the moral skeptic. For those interested in such things, I have appended a synopsis of the major arguments contained in this book, both those used to argue for skepticism, and those that have been directed against ethical objectivism.

I think that the events of the past century, culminating (as of this writing) in the unfolding tragedies of September 11, have made it quite easy, and at the same time extremely difficult, to believe in the claims that I have set forth in this book. On the one hand, the scale of the horrors that have been perpetrated within our lifetimes has made it easy to believe in a good and evil that is something other than mere personal or cultural endorsement. We have seen how individuals and societies can be very badly wrong in moral matters, even if they are incapable of noting the error of their ways. Dictators and terrorists may be perfectly sincere in their commitments, and unconvinceable to the end. But they are mistaken nonetheless.

That a fanatic is unbudgeable does not make him morally infallible. One of the attractions of ethical objectivism is its ready explanation for why that is so.

On the other hand, the increasing dominance of a scientific world view, in which there is ever greater pressure to exclude from reality anything that cannot be empirically verified, leaves little room for the normative aspect of existence. The picture of reality that we are asked to accept sees all things, including us, as constellations of atoms in the void. There is matter. There is nothingness. And that is it. Hardly any room out there for good and evil.

These world views compete for our allegiance. They cannot both be correct. Our task is difficult precisely because both are much more than superficially plausible. When we are ill and seek a cure, when we want a bountiful harvest or a reliable support system to cross a river's span, we don't want voodoo. We want science. And science hasn't anything to say about good and evil. Ask the folks in lab coats, go read their journals. They'll send you over to the philosophy department.

Despite the amazing progress of the natural sciences, we should resist any effort to straitjacket the whole of reality into borders dictated exclusively by their findings. We are not rejecting science, just placing limits on its purview. Science can only partially fix the boundaries of reality; it doesn't have the final say across the board. The natural sciences are fit to tell us about the empirical world. They are unfit to tell us about the normative world. That doesn't mean that there is no such world. It just means that science can't analyze and describe its contents.

One way to think about this is to recognize that there are specifically philosophical truths—about what (if anything) is right and wrong, about whether free will exists, about the conditions under which we might gain knowledge of reality, etc. We may remain ignorant about many of these truths, but they are certainly not of our own making. These truths are objective, and they are not ratified by science. Therefore there are nonscientific objective truths.

There is no tension in this picture, unless we are being driven by the false assumption that science must confirm all truths. Abandon that assumption, and we make room for a world that contains moral truths not of our own making. That is our world.

SYNOPSIS OF THE MAJOR ARGUMENTS

THE ARGUMENT FROM FREEDOM OF CONSCIENCE AND EXPRESSION

1. If people possess equal rights to an opinion about X, then their opinions about X are equally plausible.
2. People possess equal rights to an opinion about morality.
3. Therefore people's views about morality are all equally plausible.

The basic problem: Premise (1) is false. Though my right to an opinion about the nature of a distant galaxy, or the cellular structure of a pomegranate, is just as valid as anyone else's, that does not mean that my opinion on these matters is just as plausible as that of (say) an astronomer or a botanist.

THE ARGUMENTS FROM TOLERANCE

First Version

1. If moral skepticism is true, then we must be tolerant.
2. Moral skepticism is true.
3. Therefore we must be tolerant.

Second Version

1. If tolerance is valuable, then skepticism is true.
2. Tolerance is valuable.
3. Therefore skepticism is true.

The basic problem: If skepticism is correct, then any moral recommendation, including one of tolerance, is either untrue, or true, but only relative to each person's or society's ultimate commitments.

Sometimes these commitments advocate intolerance. It follows that if subjectivism or relativism is true, then those with such commitments are acting immorally if they are tolerant. That is too insecure a basis for establishing the value of tolerance.

THE PROOF THAT EVERYTHING FOLLOWS FROM A CONTRADICTION

"A" and "B," below, are variables that can be replaced by any declarative sentence at all—no restrictions.

1. A is true and A is false.
2. Therefore A is true.
3. Therefore either A is true or B is true.
4. A is false.
5. Therefore B is true.

Analysis

- (1) is a statement of a contradiction.
- (1) logically entails (2): A conjunction (i.e., a combination of claims) logically entails the truth of each conjunct (i.e., each of its distinct constituent claims).
- (2) logically entails (3): A true claim logically entails any disjunction (an either-or claim) with the true claim as one of its disjuncts.
- (1) logically entails (4): A conjunction logically entails the truth of each conjunct.
- (3) and (4) logically entail (5): for any true disjunction, the falsity of all but one disjunct logically entails the truth of the remaining one.
- Lesson: "B" stands for any declarative sentence at all. So a contradiction logically entails the truth of any and every claim, no matter how absurd, and no matter how unrelated to the contradiction's claims it happens to be.

THE ARGUMENT FROM GLOBAL SKEPTICISM

1. If global skepticism is true, then moral skepticism is true.
2. Global skepticism is true.
3. Therefore moral skepticism is true.

The basic problem: Though premise (1) is certainly true, premise (2) is false. Global skepticism is self-refuting. Global nihilism is clearly self-refuting. Global subjectivism refutes itself, provided anyone thinks it false (as I do). Global relativism is self-refuting in every instance in which a society's deepest commitments imply its rejection (as is the case in every actual society).

MODUS TOLLENS

Modus tollens is any argument that takes the following form:

1. If P is true, then Q is true.
2. Q is false.
3. Therefore P is false.

P and Q can be any declarative sentence at all. Every instance of this argument is logically valid, i.e., such that if all of its premises were true, then its conclusion, logically, must be true as well. It is impossible for all premises to be true and the conclusion false.

Why does modus tollens work every time? The first premise of modus tollens is a conditional (an if-then sentence). A conditional has two parts: the antecedent (the if-clause), and the consequent (the then-clause). The consequent is a necessary condition (a prerequisite, a requirement, a precondition) of the antecedent. Without its necessary underpinning, the antecedent collapses. And that is just what modus tollens tells us will happen.

THE ARGUMENT FROM DISAGREEMENT

1. If well-informed, open-minded people intractably disagree about some claim, then that claim cannot be objectively true.
2. Well-informed, open-minded people intractably disagree about all ethical claims.
3. Therefore there are no objective ethical truths.

The basic problem: Premise (1) is false. Intractable disagreement in nonmoral areas, such as physics and geology and chemistry, does not indicate a lack of objective truth. So it begs the question to assume that such disagreement entails skepticism just for ethics, when it fails to have that effect elsewhere.

Further, ethical disagreement is a species of philosophical disagreement. The presence of intractable disagreement within philosophy does not signal a lack of objective truth. There is an objective truth about whether there is a God, or free will, or good and evil, despite intractable philosophical disagreement on these issues. Absent further argument, there is every reason to offer the same diagnosis when it comes to the existence of objectively true ethical standards.

THE ARGUMENT FROM ATHEISM

1. Ethics is objective only if God exists.
2. God does not exist.
3. Therefore ethics is not objective.

The basic problems:

- Theists should reject (1), because the natural justification for (1)—the Divine Command Theory—is problematic, primarily because it yields a conception of God as an arbitrary being whose choices are unsupported by reasons.
- Atheists should reject (1), because they have, as they see it, examples of other laws (e.g., those in math, logic, physics) whose objectivity does not rest on divine authority.
- Theists will reject (2) and claim that, absent further argument, it begs the question.

THE ARGUMENT FROM OCCAM'S RAZOR

1. We have reason to believe that something exists only if it is explanatorily indispensable.
2. Moral facts are not explanatorily indispensable.
3. Therefore we lack reason to believe in the existence of moral facts.

The basic problem: Though moral facts do not explain what goes on in the world, the test that says they must, in order to earn ontological credibility, is too restrictive. Moral facts are not meant to be descriptive, are not meant to play a role in causal citations and predictions of observable phenomena, but are rather evaluative and normative. There must be some normative truths, which are not the sort of things that do any explaining, but instead guide us in how we *ought* to go on doing things. If there were no such truths, then Occam's razor, itself a normative principle, could not be true, either.

THE ARGUMENT FROM CERTAINTY

1. Knowledge requires certainty.
2. We can never be certain of the truth of our moral beliefs.
3. Therefore we can never have moral knowledge.

The basic problem: Premise (1) is either false, or it rules out the possibility of knowing anything but the most trivial truths. Thus if moral knowledge has to go, so too does knowledge about everything else, except the momentary content of one's thoughts.

THE EPISTEMIC ARGUMENT FROM DISAGREEMENT

1. If well-informed, open-minded people intractably disagree about some claim, then we cannot know whether that claim is true.
2. Well-informed, open-minded people intractably disagree about all moral claims.
3. Therefore there can be no moral knowledge.

The basic problem: Premise (1) is false. A failure to convince intelligent opponents does not necessarily undermine one's own views. If it did, then there would be no philosophical knowledge, since all philosophical claims are disputed by intelligent others. Yet if there were no philosophical knowledge, then we couldn't justifiably assess any philosophical argument, including the present one.

Further, there have been well-informed, consistent skeptical positions that attempt to cast doubt on all of our knowledge, not just that in ethics and philosophy generally. Such skepticism cannot be decisively refuted. This means that there is intractable disagreement, among very intelligent and open-minded people, about everything. Therefore, if premise (1) were true, we'd have to give up hopes of having any knowledge at all.

THE PERSPECTIVAL ARGUMENT

1. We are able to gain knowledge only if our beliefs are formed from within the best perspective for judging the matter at hand.
2. There is no best perspective from which to judge moral matters.
3. Therefore we can't have any moral knowledge.

The basic problems: Premise (2) may be false—the best moral perspective might be one in which we purge ourselves of false beliefs and gain all relevant nonmoral information, treat everyone's interests equally, judge dispassionately, etc. However, if (2) is true, then premise (1) is false. There is no single best perspective from which to make judgments about physics or philosophy, yet some such judgments are credible. It is possible that truth might be captured from a variety of equally good viewpoints, there being no best vantage point among them.

THE ARGUMENT FROM INADEQUATE EVIDENCE

1. If one knows that a claim is true, then one must have adequate evidence for that claim.
2. Adequate evidence must come in the form of empirical support.
3. There is inadequate empirical support for any moral claim.
4. Therefore there is no moral knowledge.

The basic problem: Premise (2) is false. In fact, if it were true, then we would not be justified in believing it, since there is no determinative empirical evidence that would substantiate (2). It is a philosophical claim, and as such cannot be decisively vindicated by reference to empirical evidence alone. Moral claims, being philosophical ones, are largely a priori and so not subject to empirical confirmation.

THE REGRESS ARGUMENT

1. If a moral belief is justified, then either (i) the moral belief is self-evident, or (ii) it is justified by another belief.
2. (i) is impossible: there are no self-evident moral beliefs.
3. (ii) is impossible: moral beliefs cannot be justified by other beliefs.

    (3a) Moral beliefs cannot be justified by nonmoral beliefs: this would violate Hume's is-ought thesis.

    (3b) Moral beliefs cannot be justified by other moral beliefs: this would land us in an infinite regress.

4. Therefore there are no justified moral beliefs.
5. Therefore there is no moral knowledge.

The basic problem: If this argument is sound, then it can be generalized to cover every area of knowledge. If moralists are unable to avoid an infinite regress, then so too are those with beliefs of any other sort.

Further replies:

- (1) may be mistaken. Beliefs may be justified by things other than beliefs—specifically, by the fact that they have been reliably produced.
- (2) may be mistaken: there may be self-evident moral beliefs.
- (3) may be mistaken: coherentists claim that a belief's being situated in a coherent network of beliefs, which confer support on the belief in question, and which in turn derive support from it, is enough to render a belief justified.

THE ARGUMENT FROM RATIONALITY

1. If you are morally obligated to do something, then you have good reason to do it.
2. If you have good reason to do something, then doing it must further what is important to you.
3. Therefore if you are morally obligated to do something, then doing it must further what is important to you.
4. What is important to you is a subjective matter, fixed by personal choice.
5. Therefore all of your moral obligations are fixed subjectively.

The basic problem: Though some objectivists bite the bullet and abandon (1), and others, following Plato, are willing to give up (4), my own view is that premise (2) is false. Our reasons may extend beyond what matters to us. Reasons are considerations that favor or oppose. There are considerations that favor easily aiding others in need, for instance, even if there's nothing in it for us when we do so.

GLOSSARY

ABSOLUTE An absolute moral rule is one that is never permissibly broken.

A PRIORI Knowledge is a priori just in case it is obtainable without reliance on empirical evidence.

ARBITRARINESS A failure to be supported by adequate reasons.

ATHEISM The view that God does not exist.

COHERENCE THEORY The view that one is justified in holding a belief if, and to the extent that, it coheres with one's other beliefs.

CONTINGENT Not necessarily true. A contingent truth is one that, under different circumstances, would have been false (e.g., that the United States has fifty states, or that the current British Prime Minister is a man).

CRITIQUE, EXTERNAL A criticism that does not try to demonstrate some internal inconsistency with a given viewpoint, but rather attacks its basic assumptions.

CRITIQUE, INTERNAL A criticism that confines itself to showing how the assumptions of an outlook are inconsistent with other views within that outlook.

DIVINE COMMAND THEORY The view according to which an act is morally right just because God commands it.

EGOISM, ETHICAL The doctrine that actions are morally right if and only if they best serve one's self-interest. More specifically, it is the view that there is only one basic morally relevant consideration: promotion of self-interest.

EGOISM, RATIONAL The doctrine that one has a reason to do something just in case doing it serves one's wants or interests. More specifically, it is the view that there is only one ultimate kind of reason: furthering or protecting what matters to you.

EMPIRICAL Based on the evidence of the senses.

EPISTEMIC Dealing with knowledge or justified belief.

ERROR-THEORY The kind of moral nihilism that claims that moral language tries, but always fails, to accurately describe a moral reality (there being none to describe).

MORALITY, CONVENTIONAL The moral rules that result from personal endorsement or interpersonal agreement.

MORALITY, CRITICAL The set of moral standards whose truth does not depend on personal or interpersonal ratification.

NIHILISM, MORAL The view that there is nothing that is right or wrong. Also the view that there are no moral truths. The two kinds of moral nihilism are **error-theories** and **non-cognitivism**.

NIHILISM, GLOBAL The self-refuting view that there is no truth (subjective *or* objective) at all.

NON-COGNITIVISM The kind of moral nihilism that claims that moral language does not attempt to describe anything, but instead is used to persuade, encourage, prescribe or be expressive of one's feelings. As such, moral judgments cannot be true or false.

NORMATIVE A normative fact or rule tells us what we *ought* to do.

OBJECTIVISM, ETHICAL The theory that claims that there are correct moral standards, and that these standards are true independently of what anyone, anywhere, thinks of them.

OCCAM'S RAZOR The maxim that advises us not to multiply entities or suppositions beyond necessity. According to Occam's razor, of two competing theories, each able to explain the same phenomena, the one likelier to be true is the one that employs the fewest assumptions and posits the fewest entities.

ONTOLOGY A list or theory of what exists.

PREMISES An argument's reasons, intended to support its conclusion.

RELATIVISM, CULTURAL The anthropological theory that claims that different societies have different ultimate ethical beliefs.

RELATIVISM, ETHICAL The philosophical theory that claims that an action is morally right if and only if it is permitted by the ultimate conventions of the society in which it is performed.

RELATIVISM, GLOBAL A kind of global skepticism, it is the view that a claim (moral *or* nonmoral) is true if and only if it is endorsed by a society, or follows from its ultimate commitments.

SELF-EVIDENCE The feature of being intrinsically plausible, of being evident in itself. A belief is self-evident just in case one's understanding of it is sufficient to justify belief in it.

SKEPTICISM, GLOBAL The view that there is no objective truth at all.

SKEPTICISM, MORAL   The family of philosophical theories that rejects ethical objectivism. Moral skepticism includes nihilism, ethical subjectivism, and ethical relativism. In other contexts, moral skepticism is neutral on the issue of whether there is objective moral truth, but insists that even if there is such a thing, we can never know it. (For this latter usage, see Chapters 18 and 19.)

SUBJECTIVISM, ETHICAL   The philosophical theory that claims that an action is morally right if and only if I approve of it, and a moral judgment is true if and only if it accurately reports the sentiments of the one who holds it.

SUBJECTIVISM, GLOBAL   One sort of global skepticism, it is the view that a proposition is true if and only if it is believed. All truth (moral and nonmoral) is in the eye of the beholder.

THEIST   One who believes that God exists.

UNIVERSAL   (i) endorsed by everyone; or (ii) applicable to everyone (even if they don't endorse it).

VALIDITY, LOGICAL   The feature of an argument that guarantees the truth of its conclusion, on the assumption (very possibly false) that all of its premises are true.

INDEX

Abortion (example)
  ideal observers and, 110
  moral disagreement and, 39, 42
  non-cognitivism and, 9
  scientific view of, 113
Absolutism, 62, 65–66
Agnosticism, 76
Antecedent, 139
A priori knowledge, 114, 116
Arbitrariness, 59–60
  characteristics of, 34–37
  defined, 34
  of Divine Command Theory, 80–81, 82
Argument from Atheism, 75–78, 140
Argument from Certainty, 103, 104–7, 141
Argument from Disagreement, 67–68, 74, 139–40. *See also* Moral disagreement
Argument from Freedom of Conscience and Expression, 20–21, 137
Argument from Global Skepticism, 50–54, 138–39
Argument from Inadequate Evidence, 103–4, 112–17, 142
Argument from Occam's Razor, 92–99, 140
Argument from Rationality, 128–31, 143
Arguments from Tolerance, 30–31, 137–38. *See also* Tolerance
Atheism, 23, 75–78, 140
Authored *vs.* authorless morality, 78, 82–83, 84, 86

Begging the question
  in Argument from Atheism, 140
  in Argument from Occam's Razor, 96
  in Arguments from Tolerance, 31

Circular reasoning, 122–23, 124, 125
Clitoridectomy (example), 44–45
Cogito ergo sum, 105
Coherence theory, 122–23, 125
Conditional, 87, 139
Confirmation test, 100–101
Consequent, 139
Contingent, 127
Contradiction, 60–61
  characteristics of, 38–42

defined, 38
ethical relativism and, 39–41, 42, 43–48
Conventional morality
  arbitrariness and, 36
  moral equivalence and, 19–20
  moral error and, 15–16, 17
Crime of Punishment, The (Menninger), 73
Cultural differences, 4, 8. *See also* Ethical relativism

Descartes, René, 104–7, 108
Divine Command Theory, 80–83, 84, 89, 140
Dogmatism, 12, 27–29, 58

Egoism
  ethical, 131–32
  rational, 126–33
Empirical methods, 70–71
Epistemic Argument from Disagreement, 103, 107–9, 141. *See also* Moral disagreement
Epistemic facts, 98–100
Error theory, 9, 16, 17, 23
Ethical egoism, 131–32
Ethical objectivism
  absolutism and, 62, 65–66
  arbitrariness and, 36–37, 59–60
  central beliefs, 11–12
  contradiction and, 42, 60–61
  conventional morality and, 15
  defined, 57
  dogmatism and, 27–29, 58
  moral disagreement and, 60
  moral equivalence and, 58
  moral error and, 16, 57
  moral progress and, 58
  moral skepticism problems solved by, 57–61
  position on God's existence, 75–84
  tolerance and, 30, 31–32, 33, 58–59
  universality and, 62–65
Ethical relativism, 6, 8, 53. *See also* Global relativism
  absolutism and, 66
  arbitrariness and, 35, 36
  central beliefs, 10–11
  contradiction and, 39–41, 42, 43–48
  conventional morality and, 17